Mr. Water

This publication is made possible by The Kerr Foundation Inc.

OKLAHOMA TRACKMAKER SERIES

by RONN CUPP
and BOB BURKE

Series Editor: Gini Moore Campbell
Associate Editor: Eric Dabney

ROBERT S. KERR, JR.

OKLAHOMA HERITAGE ASSOCIATION
Oklahoma City

Copyright 2005 by Oklahoma Heritage Association

All rights reserved. No part of this book may be reproduced or utilized in any form or by any means, electronic or mechanical, including photocopying and recording, by any information storage and retrieval system, without permission of the publisher.

Printed in the United States of America.
ISBN 1-88559651-0
Library of Congress Catalog Number 2005938934
Book cover and contents designed by Sandi Welch/www.2WDesignGroup.com

OKLAHOMA HERITAGE ASSOCIATION BOARD OF DIRECTORS

Roxana Lorton, Tulsa
Chairman of the Board
Glen D. Johnson, Durant
Chairman Elect
Clayton I. Bennett
Chairman Emeritus

Frederick Drummond, Pawhuska, *Vice Chairman*
Ken Fergeson, Altus, *Vice Chairman*
Gary Huckaby, Mustang, *Vice Chairman*
Larry Lee, Tulsa, *Vice Chairman*
Paul Massad, Norman, *Vice Chairman*
John Nickel, Welling, *Vice Chairman*
Meg Salyer, Oklahoma City, *Vice Chairman*
Justice Steve Taylor, McAlester, *Vice Chairman*
Becky J. Frank, Tulsa, *Secretary*
Roger Collins, Bristow, *Treasurer*

Directors
Ray Ackerman, Oklahoma City
Wanda L. Bass, McAlester
Jim Bellatti, Stillwater
G.T. Blankenship, Oklahoma City
Ed Boynton, Durant
Bob Burke, Oklahoma City
Nevyl Cable, Okmulgee
Chester Cadieux, Tulsa
Luke Corbett, Oklahoma City
Bridge Cox, Ardmore
Carol Crawford, Frederick
Betty Crow, Altus
Clyde Estes, Henryetta
John Feaver, Chickasha
Vaughndean Fuller, Tulsa
Martin D. Garber, Jr., Bartlesville
Marlin "Ike" Glass, Jr., Newkirk
C. Hubert Gragg, Newcastle
Jean Harbison, Lawton

Pat Henry, Lawton
Rick Holder, Gould
Dr. Ernest L. Holloway, Langston
William E. Humphrey, Pauls Valley
David Kyle, Tulsa
Dave Lopez, Oklahoma City
Paul Massad, Norman
John Massey, Durant
Tom J. McDaniel, Oklahoma City
J.W. McLean, Frisco, Texas
Robert P. "Bob" McSpadden, Vinita
Tom Muchmore, Ponca City
John W. Nichols, Oklahoma City
Mary Jane Noble, Ardmore
C.D. Northcutt, Ponca City
Suzanne O'Brien, Tulsa
Deane Oven, Tulsa
Leslie Paris, Tulsa
Bond Payne, Oklahoma City
Robert Poe, Tulsa
Richard Poole, Stillwater
David Rainbolt, Oklahoma City
Carl R. Renfro, Ponca City
Sharon Shoulders, Henryetta
Lee Allan Smith, Oklahoma City
G. Lee Stidham, Checotah
Harold C. Stuart, Jensen Beach, FL
Chuck Thompson, Norman
Blake Wade, Oklahoma City
Peter M. Walter, Tulsa
Myra B. Ward, Enid

OKLAHOMA HERITAGE ASSOCIATION
201 Northwest Fourteenth Street
Oklahoma City, Oklahoma 73103

ACKNOWLEDGMENTS 5

FOREWORD *by Luke R. Corbett* 7

Chapter 1 **A ROBUST ANCESTRY** 9

Chapter 2 **A LEGACY BEGINS** 21

Chapter 3 **LAND, WOOD, AND WATER** 51

Chapter 4 **LEARNING THE ROPES** 65

Chapter 5 **BEARING THE BURDEN** 87

Chapter 6 **LIGHTING A NEW TORCH** 97

Chapter 7 **WATER CHAMPION** 113

Chapter 8 **LOU** 137

Chapter 9 **THE GLOVER DEBATE** 149

Chapter 10 **DEVELOPING A WATER PLAN** 165

Chapter 11 **WATER FOR ECONOMIC DEVELOPMENT** 177

Chapter 12 **QUEST FOR THE SENATE** 191

Chapter 13 **THE 1980 WATER PLAN** 211

Chapter 14 **AN ACTIVE ADVOCATE** 233

ENDNOTES 257

INDEX 263

MANY PEOPLE GRACIOUSLY HELPED in gathering photographs and information for this book. Bob Kerr, Jr.'s life could not have adequately been told without the assistance of Bob's widow, Lou Kerr; his children, Robert S. Kerr, III, Shari Kerr, Cody Kerr, Bill Kerr, Valerie Kerr Hart, Steve Kerr, and Laura Kerr Ogle; and his sister and brothers, Kay Kerr Adair, Bill Kerr, and Breene Kerr. A special insight into Bob's early years was provided by his cousin, Jim Anderson.

Thanks to Karen Horton, Cecilia Castle Miller, Dwayne Thornton, Georgia Fiering, and Anne Holzberlein for editorial assistance. George and Marcia Davis assisted our editors, Gini Moore Campbell and Eric Dabney, in proofreading the manuscript.

We appreciate the efforts of Linda Lynn, Melissa Hayer, Mary Phillips, Robin Davison, and Billie Harry at the Oklahoma Publishing Company for help in selecting photographs; Amy Clakley and Debbie Neill for transcribing interviews; Sandi Welch for her wonderful design of both the dust jacket and interior of the book; and the Oklahoma Heritage Association and its chair, Roxana Lorton, and director of publications and education, Gini Moore Campbell, for their commitment to preserve Oklahoma's great history.

Foreword

BY LUKE R. CORBETT

For nearly 40 years, Robert S. Kerr, Jr. served on the board of directors of Kerr-McGee Corporation. During those years, he demonstrated the same level of commitment, the same passion for excellence, and the same devotion to Oklahoma that characterized the service of his father, Robert S. Kerr, Sr., a co-founder of Kerr-McGee in 1929.

When I met Bob Kerr, Jr., as a member of the Kerr-McGee Board of Directors, I was a newcomer both to the company and the state. Even so, it did not take long to appreciate Bob's acumen as a businessman and attorney, and his integrity as a person.

This biography of Bob chronicles his tireless efforts to develop water resources in Oklahoma. The story of those efforts, and the impact they have made on the state's economy, image, and quality of life, reinforces how one man can make a significant contribution to his native state.

Mr. Water includes historical material about Bob, his illustrious father, business legends such as Dean A. McGee, and the company they grew into one of the leading U.S.-based independent oil and natural gas exploration and production firms.

Almost every state in America has been graced by a family whose leadership and vision were fundamental to the state's development and prosperity. In Oklahoma, that family was the Kerrs. This book offers new insights into the Kerr family influence, which extended from the board room to the United States Senate chamber, as well as its legacy of public service that continues to reach far beyond the borders of Oklahoma.

—LUKE R. CORBETT
Chairman and CEO, Kerr-McGee Corporation

A ROBUST ANCESTRY

ROBERT SAMUEL KERR, JR., was born from a bloodline of survival, courage, and leadership. His ancestral family tree is filled with tales of failure, disaster, murder, hard times, and finally, success. The rugged American frontier was not kind to the Kerr ancestors—only a few families suffered as much bloodshed and misery as them. However, they endured and produced statesmen, traders, stonecutters, grain millers, surveyors, lawyers, engineers, and explorers.[1]

Four hundred years before the name Bob Kerr would strike fear in the hearts of political opponents in America, Sir Robert Kerr, warden of the middle Marches of Scotland, was murdered during a riot in 1511. His sons violently expressed their vengeance by killing their father's murderer in his bed.[2]

> I was fortunate to be brought into the world into a family that expected their children to do their best and give back to the community.
>
> —ROBERT S. KERR, JR.

The Kerrs left Scotland for America in the early years of the 18th century after the Scots were defeated by the English in the Battle of Culloden in 1707. As English troops hunted down and slaughtered Highlanders, the Kerrs and their neighbors had a choice—they could starve, join the British Army, or leave for the New World.

At least one of the Kerr ancestors, William Thornton, could trace his lineage to the English royal family, particularly William the Conqueror, King Henry I, and King Edward I. Thornton emigrated to Virginia before 1641. He was followed to America by other Kerr kin, including William Winston, who was also the great great grandfather of American patriot Patrick Henry.[3]

Bob Jr.'s 7th great grandfather was James Taylor, a distant cousin of two American presidents, James Madison and Zachary Taylor. Several branches of Bob Jr.'s family launched their fortunes by tilling the rich soil of Virginia, Maryland, Tennessee, and South Carolina before moving west.[4]

The direct Kerr line began in a calm manner when John Kerr left Belfast, Ireland, in 1825 and sailed with his wife and 20-year-old son, William Edward Kerr, to the United States. William Edward "Big Bill" Kerr, Bob Jr.'s great grandfather, was born in South Carolina in 1838 before his father picked up his stake and traversed the Appalachians into the new frontier in Tennessee.

In the 1850s, Big Bill selected a home site in the tangled, wooden swamps of Fulton County in northern Arkansas. Clearing land with an axe in one hand and watching for bears and wolves with a gun in the other was a daily routine for Kerr and for his future in-laws, the Fore family, that settled the remote and primitive country of southern Missouri, in the heart of the Ozarks.[5]

Missouri had been admitted to the Union as a slave state, so the Kerrs and Fores joined many Missourians in enlisting in the Confederate Army to fight for southern principles in the Civil

War. Missouri was hard hit by the War Between the States. Flames consumed entire towns and thousands of acres of essential crops. Bob Jr.'s great great grandfather, Sam Fore, and his son, Jim, were shot down by northern sympathizers while they pressed tobacco leaves grown on their Missouri farm.

Big Bill Kerr joined Company C, First Missouri Regiment, Volunteers, Confederate States of America, and fought as a private in the ranks, sometimes without a gun. When he came home, he married Margaret "Maggie" Fore, born in 1844, and built a home in extreme southern Missouri at Bennett's Bayou. A son, William Samuel "Sam" Kerr, was born in 1868 in Bakersfield, Missouri. When Sam was only nine months old, another Kerr family tragedy happened.[6]

The Kerrs were caught in the middle of violence and revenge as the slavery issue reared its ugly head with the Ku Klux Klan clashing with old enemies. During the middle of the night, Big Bill was gunned down by a mob as he crawled through the front door of his cabin, desperate to protect his wife and child from stray bullets. Townspeople built a homemade coffin, but Big Bill was too large for it. Nearly a year later, family members gathered to pay proper respects to him. The community responded to Big Bill's cowardly murder and opened their arms and hearts to his widow and child.[7]

Sadness overtook the Kerr line again when Sam Kerr was orphaned at age five—his mother died in childbirth after remarrying. Sam went to live with his mother's sister, Mary Mitchell, on a farm in Baxter County, Arkansas. Until he reached adulthood at age 18, Sam worked, fished, and swam in the bayou nestled among the Ozark hills.

Sam, Bob Jr.'s grandfather, took life seriously and spent much of his teenage years reading, thinking, and wanting to become a lawyer. Knowing that liquor had played a part in his father's murder a generation before, Sam publicly declared his stand against alcohol and the destruction he had seen it cause. Still a teenager, Sam was able to buy his half-brother's interest in the family farm and began to raise crops on Bennett's Bayou.[8]

Sam's tee-totaler convictions ran afoul of his adopted parents' family and the murderous bands around West Plains, Missouri. Everyone, it seemed, carried a gun. Sam took the code of frontier justice seriously and openly talked of revenging his father's death. But in truth, he had loftier dreams. He set his eye on studying law and worked hard to obtain enough money to put himself through law school.

He knew his place was no longer in Missouri, so in 1888, at age 19, he packed his few worldly goods in a covered wagon and headed south to Texas. He crossed northern Arkansas to Fort Smith and then veered southwest along the Butterfield Trail, an overland mail route that had been abandoned during the Civil War.[9]

Sam liked the unspoiled land he saw in Indian Territory as he drove his wagon to Boggy Depot and on to Colbert's Ferry to cross the Red River into Texas. He ventured 100 miles into Texas, looking for work in Ellis County. His plans were to find work in the farming community of Milford, save enough money to attend college at the University of Texas, and send back to Missouri for his sweetheart, Artie Hall.[10]

Ellis County was the home to another family that would greatly impact the future of Oklahoma. Only a few miles from where Sam lived, William Boren grew cotton in the fertile land. Boren was the father of Oklahoma Congressman Lyle H. Boren and grandfather of David L. Boren who served Oklahoma as governor, United States senator, and president of the University of Oklahoma.

Sam found life in Texas harder than expected. Cotton was king in Ellis County, and bumper crops were harvested in the

William Samuel "Sam" Kerr was born in Missouri in 1868. He moved first to Texas, then to Ada, Indian Territory, in 1895.

Sam Kerr lived with his aunt and uncle, Rube and Mary Mitchell, from the time he was five until age 19. *Courtesy James K. Anderson.*

rich bottom lands. But farm labor earned him only $12 to $20 monthly. He was certain he could do better, especially if he could find a country school that would hire him as a teacher. He wrote home on April 15, 1888, "It is a much nicer place and is much more agreeable when it is dry and I believe if I can get a school this fall, I can do much better here than I can there."[11]

Times were hard also in Missouri, and Sam's farm did not readily sell. With his life in limbo, his fiancée, Artie Hall, grew impatient. She married another man on Christmas Day, 1889. Sam tried to quiet his disappointment by borrowing money to live on while he waited for his Missouri land to sell. He taught school for awhile near Milford, Texas.

In the fall of 1891 he reported to members of his remaining family in Missouri that he earned $100 picking cotton. Looking for innovative ways to earn money, Sam bought a race horse with visions of winning cash prizes. At one race in Milford, he caught the eye of his future wife.[12]

Margaret Churchel "Maggie" Wright was fun loving and had been picking cotton with friends to have enough money to go to the state fair in Dallas. She told a girlfriend that the young horseman with long brown sideburns and a flowing mustache was hers.

Maggie had been raised "proper," so Sam had to make the first move if the couple was to have any future. Sam formally requested his first date with Maggie in a handwritten note, stating, "Compliments of W.S. Kerr to Miss Maggie Wright and would be pleased to have the honor of calling at one o'clock P.M. Sunday, January 31."[13]

Sam arrived at Maggie's home wearing a light gray Prince Albert coat and a black bow tie. They rode unchaperoned into the countryside in Sam's buggy. As they talked, they found their childhoods had been equally full of turmoil and sadness. Maggie's father, Moses Leonard Wright, a former Confederate soldier, had been killed while serving on a posse looking for horse thieves. Maggie's mother, Fannie Taylor Wright, remarried, and the family lived for awhile in Indian Territory before returning to Ellis County.[14]

Sam and Maggie did not immediately get married. Sam was still focused on education. Back in Missouri, Sam's uncle, Polk Hall, who had loaned Sam money with the family farm as collateral, was worried that Sam had been living in Texas for more than three years and still had not found a bride. Sam wrote Hall on March 14, 1892, only a little more than a month after his first date with Maggie, "Now, as to your advice concerning marriage, I will say that I appreciate it and thank you for your interest you manifest in my future life, but I will not promise that I will heed it, for if I can sell what little I possess in Missouri, I am going to attend school for at least 4 years."[15]

Sam told his uncle by marriage that if he could sell his Missouri farm he would enroll in the college at nearby Italy, Texas, for a year and then attend "one of the leading Eastern universities and take a complete Classical course and then a thorough course in Law."[16]

Sam also expressed interest in making an extensive tour of Europe to "better acquaint himself with the political methods and social customs of foreign nations." His sturdy Kerr constitution showed in the closing paragraph of the letter, "This may seem like a lot of foolishness to you, but I am cranky enough to entertain such ideas and will attempt to put them into execution if I can only turn my property into money."[17]

Sam and Maggie were married on December 14, 1893, in nearby Waco, Texas. After a brief honeymoon, they returned to set up housekeeping in Milford. Their first quarrel was over Maggie's white cat sleeping with them. Sam firmly declared, "I love you better than anything in all the world, but either that cat or I will

Margaret Churchel "Maggie" Wright married Sam Kerr in 1893. She became known as "Grandmother Kerr" and was the matriarch of the Kerr family in Ada.

have to leave this bed." "Willie," as Maggie called Sam, won, and the cat was forced to find a sleeping place elsewhere. Sam wrote Uncle Polk, "I am a happy married man…Was married on the 14th and have begun the battles of life in earnest."[18]

Maggie was strong willed, but her good humor balanced Sam's sober and introspective mannerisms. She encouraged her new husband's lingering wish to study law. She worked with him to use all their resources to plant a big cotton crop in the spring of 1894. If he realized the profit they expected, they could travel to a major university town, and Sam could become the lawyer he had wanted to be since childhood.

Circumstances beyond his control squashed Sam's dream for higher education. A national panic broke the cotton market and wiped out the young family's savings. Instead of moving toward the University of Texas, Sam and Maggie looked northward to Indian Territory. He remembered how much he liked the wilderness. Also, he had heard stories how Indian land could be leased for practically nothing if it was developed for crops.

Sam retraced his steps to Indian Territory alone. He left Maggie nursing a new baby, Lois Frances Kerr, born January 18, 1895. The plan was for Sam to find a place to live, build a cabin, and return for his wife and child. Traveling the Old Texas Road in a wagon loaded with tools and supplies, Sam crossed the Red river and drove to Boggy Depot, a major trading center of the Choctaw Nation.

From Boggy Depot, Sam turned northwest. When he stopped to check his horses a few miles south of the Indian trading post of Ada, he took in the grandeur of the rolling hills and wooded vales of Pecan Valley. Sam saw everything he needed—land, wood, and water. He needed good land to grow crops, wood to build a cabin, barn, and fences, and water to sustain his family and livestock.[19]

Ada was named for Ada Reed, daughter of William J. Reed, the first postmaster of the Ada post office that was established July 10, 1891. Ada was the Record Town for Recording District No. 16 of Indian Territory and, at statehood, became the county seat of Pontotoc County.

Sam leased 160 acres from Amos Hayes, a Chickasaw Indian, on February 28, 1895. The parcel of land was rugged and beautiful, but it would take years of backbreaking labor of uprooting huge trees and breaking the hard ground to prepare enough land to grow sufficient crops to keep his family from going hungry. He quickly built a tent house with a dirt floor and boarded at the sides.

In the spring, as Pecan Valley was covered with pink and white dogwood blossoms, Sam sent for Maggie and Lois. They were coming by train to Boggy Depot, the nearest railroad to Ada. It took Sam three days to make the journey by wagon.

Sam could hardly wait to show his wife their new home. They crossed through thick stands of virgin timber, both evergreen and flowering deciduous species. The wagon forded clear, blue streams of sparkling water. Wild flowers painted the wide open spaces in a dozen different hues, a magnificent backdrop to the sounds of the wilderness, birds and animals unaccustomed to human visitors.

Maggie set up housekeeping in the tent house, thankful for the shelter in the pristine woods. Soon, Sam began building a log cabin on land he cleared on a small knoll surrounded by deep woods. The cabin was 14 feet square, made of notched logs with no windows and a single door. He hand-cut the shingles to cover the cabin and a small front porch.

The Kerrs moved into the new cabin in the summer of 1896. It was none too soon because Maggie was expecting another baby. Sam wanted a boy—and a boy he got. Robert Samuel Kerr weighed 11 pounds when he was born on September 11, 1896.

Sam was extremely proud of his son. He wrote his Uncle Polk, "My life is now everything but what I once anticipated." With crops flourishing in his newly cleared fields, and a loving wife taking care of his two babies, Sam was on top of the world, especially now that he had a son bearing his name.

A LEGACY BEGINS

ROBERT SAMUEL KERR, SR., (RSK) arrived in Ada in the same year as rail service. The once isolated Indian trading post was connected to the world when Congress authorized the building of a line connected to the Sapulpa-Oklahoma City line.

Within the next four years, RSK had two younger siblings, Mildred Margaret "Millie Muff" Kerr, born in 1898, and Aubrey Moke Kerr, born in 1900. The family moved nearer the town of Ada where Sam became a cotton buyer and merchant. The new Kerr home in town was close to a subscription school where RSK began the first grade in 1901, for the whopping sum of $1.50 per month. A third Kerr son, Travis Mitchell, was born in 1902.

At statehood, Sam Kerr was elected the first county clerk of Pontotoc County. His 11-year-old son, RSK, accompanied Sam on the trek around the county, enlisting the help

> *Bob Jr. was a quiet kid. He was kind and patient with his brothers and sister.*
> —BREENE KERR

of his neighbors in the campaign. Sam taught his son the value of public service.

RSK picked cotton and peddled fruit to save enough money to pay tuition at East Central Normal School in Ada. However, Sam and Maggie wanted their oldest son to attend the new Baptist university in Shawnee. Oklahoma Baptist University (OBU) was opening classes to not only future preachers, but any student who wanted a quality, religious-based education. The whole family took outside jobs and pooled their money to send both Lois and RSK to OBU. However, when OBU temporarily suspended classes, RSK returned to Ada where he graduated from East Central Normal School in 1913.

RSK's teaching certificate allowed him to be a school teacher in any district that would hire him. He finished out the term of a rural school before turning his attention to his father's peach orchards. Soon, he began living his father's dream of attending college and law school by borrowing money and enrolling at the University of Oklahoma. However, after a year, the money ran out and RSK left school for the final time.[1]

After serving as a second lieutenant in the United States Army field artillery in Europe in World War I, RSK returned home and married Reba Shelton on December 5, 1919. Two years later, their twin girls died at birth. RSK operated a produce business for awhile until fire destroyed his business and left him $10,000 in debt. The catastrophe forced him to turn to law, his youthful ambition.[2]

RSK accepted an invitation from Ada attorney J.F. McKeel to study law. After 11 months of watching Judge McKeel in the courtroom, and studying stacks of law books, RSK passed the Oklahoma bar examination and was admitted to practice law. He also joined the Oklahoma National Guard and became a charter member of the Ada post of the American Legion. He was a popular speaker at civic clubs and church outings.

One of the dark chapter's in RSK's life began in February, 1924, when his wife and a baby boy died in childbirth. RSK lived alone for nearly two years, writing melancholy poetry to his departed wife and three children. He also became heavily involved in the American Legion, rising to the rank of state commander.

Then, he spotted a tall, blond girl, Grayce Breene, playing tennis. Grayce, from Tulsa, was scheduled to address the Ada Lions Club. RSK arranged to sit with Grayce at the head table at the meeting. The bashful country lawyer stumbled through an attempted conversation until he mentioned horses. Grayce, born September 12, 1900, was an accomplished horsewoman. Moving quickly, RSK invited her for an afternoon ride. On their third date, RSK informed Grayce they were going to be married.[3]

RSK borrowed $1,000 and made the necessary arrangements to marry Grayce in Tulsa the day after Christmas, 1925. As his fortunes turned merrier after the tragedy of his first marriage, RSK dubbed Grayce "Lady Luck."

Grayce was the daughter of Harry and Blanche Breene, a prominent Tulsa oil family. Harry Breene had followed the lure of oil from Oil City, Pennsylvania, to Oklahoma. Grayce's life in Ada was a far cry from her upbringing in Tulsa, the glittering, high-society oil capital of the world, and nearby Bartlesville. As a young woman, she had dated author Ernest Hemingway and was talented in many ways. She studied the languages of European opera, was a trained and accomplished soprano, and a natural on the piano.

The new couple's religions were quite different—he was a staunch, tee-totaler Baptist, and she was a practicing Christian Scientist.[4]

Practicing law in Ada was not giving RSK the wealth he wanted for his family, so he turned to the oil business in 1926. He earlier had told his father that he had three goals in life—to have a family, make a million dollars, and be elected governor of his native Oklahoma. RSK's father replied, "Be sure and accomplish the first two goals before pursuing the third."

By going to work for Dixon Brothers, an oil and gas drilling concern in Anadarko, Oklahoma, RSK followed the path of his brother-in-law, James Leroy "Jim" Anderson, the company's chief field man. Anderson was married to RSK's sister, Mildred.

ABOVE: Robert S. Kerr married Grayce Breene in Tulsa on December 26, 1925.

LEFT: Grandmother Kerr with five of her six children. Left to right, Aubrey M. Kerr, Billy B. Kerr, Lois Wimberley, Grandma Kerr, Robert S. Kerr, and Travis M. Kerr. *Courtesy Oklahoma Publishing Company.*

This photograph of the Kerr in-laws was taken on the front porch of the Kerr home in Ada in the early 1930s. Front row, left to right, Jewell Kerr and Gerry Kerr. Back row, left to right, James L. Anderson, Grayce Kerr, and Carl Wimberley. At back is Grandmother Cantwell, the mother of Grandmother Kerr. *Courtesy James K. Anderson.*

RSK and Grayce began their family with the birth of Robert Samuel Kerr, Jr., (Bob, Jr.) in Ada on October 25, 1926. A second child, Breene Mitchell Kerr, was born January 27, 1929. It was also the year RSK and Jim Anderson bought Dixon Brothers for $5,000 cash and a $25,000 mortgage. The new company was called Anderson & Kerr Drilling Company. The company later

ABOVE: Bob Jr. on horseback outside the two-story home built by RSK in Ada. When RSK and Grayce moved to Oklahoma City, the home was purchased by RSK's brother, Aubrey.

BELOW: Sam Kerr, left, in front of the log cabin near Ada where most of his children were born. To his left are Maggie Kerr, Jewell Kerr, Moni Kerr, and Aubrey Kerr. *Courtesy James K. Anderson.*

A LEGACY BEGINS **27**

ABOVE: Left to right, Moni Kerr; Sarah Frances Cantwell, Maggie Kerr's mother; Sam Kerr; and Maggie Kerr. In front are Jim Anderson, left, and Robert S. Kerr, Jr. Looking around Bob Jr. is Breene Kerr. *Courtesy James K. Anderson.*

LEFT: Robert S. Kerr, left, began in the oil business with his brother-in-law, James Leroy "Jim" Anderson, right, field man for an oil well drilling company. *Courtesy James K. Anderson.*

would be known as Kerr-McGee Corporation, after RSK joined forces with young geologist, Dean McGee, who had made his mark in the oil fields by convincing his bosses where to strike oil in the Oklahoma City Field. By age 31, McGee was the chief geologist for Phillips Petroleum.[5]

Two more children were added to the RSK family in the 1930s. Grayce Kay was born in Ada on May 25, 1931, and William

Graycen Kerr was born in Oklahoma City, October 18, 1937. Because RSK was successful in the oil business, his family did not suffer greatly during the Great Depression.

Robert S. Kerr, Jr., right, and his brother, Breene.

The Kerrs were a typical family in the 1930s—RSK was the head of the household, and Grayce was a tall, beautiful, talented, charming, supportive, and creative wife. "Mother loved dogs, her children, oriental art, floral table linens and fine china, and her life-long confident, her sister-in-law Jewel Kerr," remembered daughter, Kay. Grayce was trained in voice and piano, both in classical music and opera.6

Breene said of his mother, "She had a good mind and a high energy level. Seldom without a project, she was able to work long hours, gardening, planting trees and bushes, baking and cooking, scouting the country side for antiques or other fixtures for her home in Oklahoma or the summer property in Minnesota."7

The property in Minnesota took on a life of its own. In early 1938, RSK and Grayce, in partnership with Aubrey and Jewell Kerr, purchased property in Minnesota surrounded on three sides by Pelican Lake. Even though a contractor was hired to develop the property, Grayce and Jewell took charge and oversaw the building of a cabin, pump house, laundry house, and bunk house that contained room for the many guests who would visit the Kerrs over the years. At first, there was plumbing only to the main cabin.

The Kerrs named the summer home, Northhome. It was a June to Labor Day respite from the hot, humid summers of Oklahoma City. As soon as the school-age children were recessed for the summer, Grayce loaded their clothing, supplies, a maid, and the family dog into a station wagon and drove two and a half days to the Minnesota woods. Only a few times during the summer would Grayce and her sister-in-law, Jewel, travel to Minneapolis to restock the food and supply cabinets at Northhome.8

ABOVE: The beauty of Cimino Bay, the Minnesota home of the Kerrs.

RIGHT: Basswood Lodge in Minnesota was an early favorite fishing spot for the Kerr family. Left to right, Lowell Clark, Bob Jr., and Robert S. Kerr, Sr. In front is Robert S. Kerr, III.

ABOVE: Bob Jr. and his father, Robert S. Kerr, Sr., after a bountiful fishing trip at their Minnesota summer home.

Content with progress on the buildings, Grayce set out to line the point on the lake with pine trees. Even though the water table was only slightly beneath the ground, she commandeered sons Bob Jr. and Breene to fill buckets with water from the lake and water the trees daily.9

As Bob Jr. and his siblings matured, they greatly appreciated Northhome for its unlimited fishing and boating opportunities and valuable family time. As RSK's business interests became more complicated, he often drove 15 miles into Brainerd, Minnesota, to place telephone calls to Oklahoma City to keep current with business developments.

RSK was a modest Baptist. Even when swimming with his children in Pelican Lake, he donned a tank top bathing suit and usually wore long pants when he hoed the family garden near the road that led to the family cabins that sprang up as RSK's siblings joined the Kerr family compound. Bob Jr. especially liked the times when Northhome was full of aunts, uncles, and cousins. It was then that his mother and her sisters-in-law prepared huge, home-cooked feasts.

RSK was patient with his children in teaching them how to fish. He considered it important that all the children, even daughter, Kay, know the intricacies of "setting the hook" and deftly retrieving a fish from the cool waters of Pelican Lake. Patience was a hallmark of RSK as he taught his children—he chose persuasion over autocratic authority.

Bob Jr. enjoyed fishing on sand bars south and east of Mooso Bay. He sometimes caught a lot of fish during full moon nights, figuring the light stimulated the feeding instinct of the Walleye Pike.10

Once while fishing with his father, Bob Jr. hooked what he thought was a small fish off Sunset Bay. As he reeled in the catch, he realized he had a "weighty" opponent. As the fish came to

Grayce Kerr, left, with Bob Jr. and his sister, Kay, at Northhome. *Courtesy Kay Kerr Adair.*

ABOVE: Bob Jr., center, and two of his friends lounge on a boat on Pelican Lake. *Courtesy Kay Kerr Adair.*

RIGHT: Birch trees rise to the sky at Pelican Lake. *Courtesy Kay Kerr Adair.*

the surface, the one-and-half-pounder was partially in the mouth of a 25 to 30-pound Great Northern Pike who reluctantly gave up his catch.[11]

Transportation around the Minnesota property was in a vintage Ford station wagon nicknamed "Old Blue," that often had to be primed by pouring gasoline directly into the carburetor. Once, when Gene Clark and a friend were starting the car, the engine caught fire. A shovel of sand smothered the flames, but Old Blue sucked the sand into every moving part. Old Blue never fully recovered.[12]

Bob Jr. also learned to handle a sail boat during his early summers at Pelican Lake. The only time he capsized was when a pretty, young girl, Pat Brower, drew his attention away from his job of keeping the boat upright.[13]

"Bob Jr. was a quiet kid," his brother, Breene remembered, "He wasn't loud like other kids. He was thoughtful, patient, and kind to his younger brothers and sister." The only time Breene could recall that Bob Jr. was not a quiet kid was once when he used extreme measures to settle down his friends after they came in for a nap following an early morning fishing trip. When the

boys grew louder, Bob Jr. entered the bedroom with a World War II German luger. Breene said, "He took out the pistol and laid a shot about eight inches over their noses in a row down that side of the guest house." The boys quickly settled down.[14]

Many famous people visited the Kerrs in Minnesota, including Oklahoma A & M President Henry Bennett; state school superintendent, Dr. A.L. Crable; and Dr. Catherrine Brudia, the female physician who attended the births of all four of Grayce Kerr's children. Dr. Brudia's favorite fishing apparel was lace-up boots, jodpurs, a shirt, and a campaign hat. "From a distance," Kay Kerr Adair remembered, "you might not know that the fisherperson on the shore was a woman, but we knew this was the woman our mother trusted to deliver her babies."[15]

President Bennett was Grayce's favorite house guest. He was wise, with a philosophical turn of mind. He arrived in the summer of 1944 to help RSK write his keynote speech for the Democratic National Convention. Bennett was always up very early in the morning, what he called "just the peep of dawn." He advised the Kerr children on fishing, saying, "You must have a drop of sweet anise on your minnow." He also advised RSK and Grayce on where he thought their children should attend school.[16]

While shouting across the bay, the Kerr children discovered the intriguing qualities of an echo. Kay Kerr Adair remembered, "We were surprised and wondered about the muted voice bouncing back off of the wooded hill that rises up from the west side of Cimino Bay. As children we shouted and hooted sometimes."[17]

Cimino Bay was the source of the name of one of the Kerr's favorite dogs. Grayce, who was the true dog lover in the family, was driving down the road one day with her sister-in-law and dear friend, Jewel, when she saw a mixed-breed dog she had to have. She drove to a farmhouse and asked the dog's owner how much he wanted for the animal. When he said, "two-fifty," Grayce thought he meant $250. She was relieved when she discovered he meant $2.50. Grayce bought the dog which stayed with the Kerr family for many years.[18]

RSK began family meals with the table blessing he learned from his parents. He was proud of his upbringing and shared his experiences with his children. These included his interests in cowboy movies, mystery stories, humor, fishing, and his views on the Bible. "He was a keen interpreter of the Scriptures," Kay remembered, "He was more interested in practical moral wisdom to be gleaned from Jesus' parables than researching historical or theological subtleties." RSK taught his children by example about balancing opposing views and interests, being tolerant of differences, respecting human potential, and "holding on" in hard times.[19]

RSK practiced what he preached on respecting differences. He had no problem with Grayce attending twice weekly testimonial services at the Christian Science church on North Robinson Avenue in Oklahoma City on Sunday mornings at the same time he was teaching Sunday school across the street at First Baptist Church. RSK and Grayce respected each other's beliefs.

Home for the Kerrs in Oklahoma City was a rambling, one-story, sandstone house that had once been a country fishing lodge. It was located on State Street, now Coltrane Road, three and half miles east and a mile north of the State Capitol. The country house, located on 40 acres, was adjacent to a large pond. Grayce had suggested the lodge be converted into a home after her husband purchased the property for entertaining business guests on fishing trips.[20]

A Mr. and Mrs. Malone lived in an older farmhouse on the property, which was operated as a real farm. The Malones gathered eggs, milked cows, and looked after the farm. One of Kay Kerr Adair's earliest memories of the home on State Street was sitting under the piano with her dog, Cimino.[21]

LEFT: Bob Jr. enjoyed hunting as well as fishing. He loved living on the wooded acreage on State Street, now Coltrane Road, in northeast Oklahoma City. *Courtesy Oklahoma Publishing Company.*

Bob Jr. stacking pulled weeds on the acreage in northeast Oklahoma City in 1940.

James K. "Jim" Anderson, left, and Bob Jr. feign a fight on the front lawn of the Anderson home in the Bush Hills section of Oklahoma City. *Courtesy James K. Anderson.*

The oldest Kerr grandchildren, "The Three Musketeers," left to right, Jim Anderson, Margaret "Moni" Kerr Boylan, and Bob Jr. at Moni's 75th birthday celebration.

While Grayce managed the household, RSK organized family travel when the children were young. There were occasional overnight trips by train to Chicago, Illinois, and frequent journeys by car to Ada for Sunday dinner with RSK's parents and other family members.[22]

Bob Jr. was introduced to strict Baptist beliefs when he visited his grandparents in Ada. Grandmother Kerr preached against card-playing, drinking, smoking, and other evils from which she desperately wanted her grandchildren to refrain. RSK was an honest tee-totaler, but Bob Jr., even in his teenage years, did not completely agree with his father's belief on abstinence from alcohol.

Bob Jr. was the third Kerr grandchild. Margaret "Moni" Kerr and James K. "Jim" Anderson were older. There were several years difference between the three oldest grandchildren and the others, causing the family to refer to Bob Jr., Moni, and Jim as "The Three Musketeers."[23]

Jim and Moni remembered large family gatherings at Grandmother Kerr's house in Ada. He said, "She was a wonderful cook and reveled in the fact that her kids and grandkids would visit her and Grandfather Kerr. She was happiest when every member of the family was there."[24]

Moni, who lived only a few miles from Grandmother Kerr's house, longed for times when she and her cousins slipped off to attend Sunday afternoon movies, although they could not reveal the fact to their strict grandmother.[25]

"Bob Jr. loved to tease," Moni remembered, "but he knew how far he could go with Jimmy and me, since we were older. He was sweet and only got involved in mischief when we led him in that direction."[26]

In his childhood, Bob Jr. grew very close to his mother. Even though he respected his father's religious beliefs, he was greatly influenced by his mother's teaching about Christian Science, a religion that traced its beginnings to Mary Baker Eddy, who turned to the Bible after being severely injured in a fall in 1866. When she was immediately healed, Eddy began a search for Scriptures to understand the principle behind her healing. She named her discovery Christian Science and explained it in 1875 when she published *Science and Health with Key to the Scriptures.* Christian Scientists believe that healing comes through scientific prayer, or spiritual communion with God. Official publications explain, "A transformation or spiritualization of a patient changes his condition."[27]

For his high school education, Bob Jr. was enrolled at the New Mexico Military Institute (NMMI) in Roswell, New Mexico, partly because his cousin, Jim Anderson, was there. When Bob Jr. was in the eighth grade, he visited Anderson at NMMI and liked the school.

Bob Jr., right, on a visit with his cousin, Jim Anderson, at the New Mexico Military Institute. Later Bob Jr. followed in his cousin's footsteps by attending the school. *Courtesy James K. Anderson.*

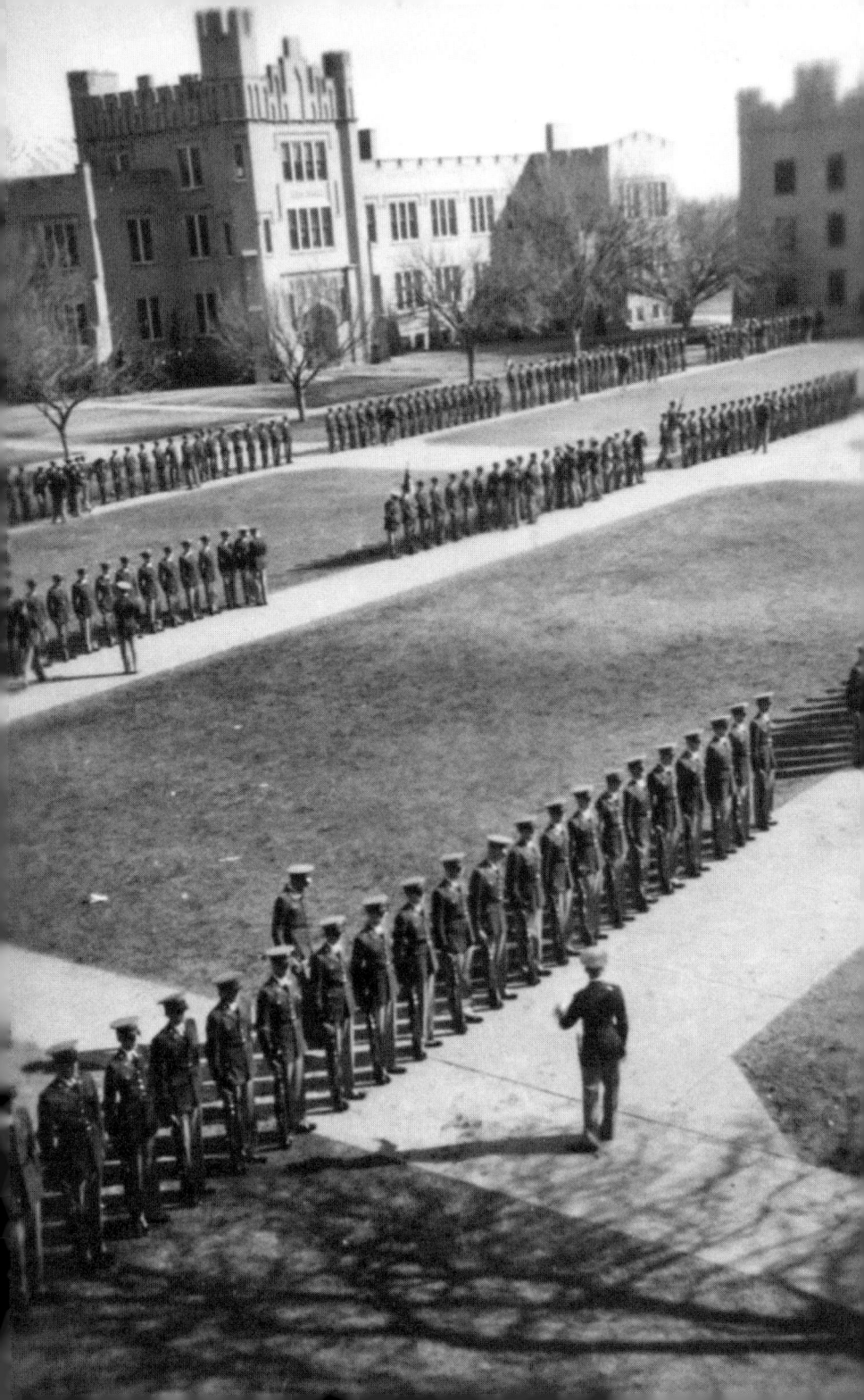

Bob Jr. attended high school at the New Mexico Military Institute in Roswell, New Mexico. *Courtesy James K. Anderson.*

Bob Jr.'s mother preferred that he attend high school at The Principia, a private Christian Science college located 40 miles from St. Louis, Missouri, on 200-foot limestone bluffs covering 2,800 acres overlooking the Mississippi, Illinois, and Missouri rivers. The school was founded by Mary Kimball Morgan, a follower of Christian Science founder Mary Baker Eddy.[28]

Bob Jr. considered attending The Principia, but was concerned about the rigid lifestyle requirements at the school. He enjoyed attending parties with his friends in Oklahoma City and did not see himself as a serious Christian Scientist, especially at age 14.[29]

Bob Jr. arrived at NMMI to begin his ninth grade studies. The school was founded in 1891 and was considered one of the nation's best college preparatory high schools in a military setting. The school, which provided training for the last three years of high school and the first two years of junior college, has been recognized since 1909 by the federal government as an "honor" military school.[30]

First year students at NMMI were referred to as "rabbits" or "rats," and were subjected to severe hazing. Jim Anderson was two years ahead of Bob Jr. and served as his cousin's corporal and first sergeant in successive years. Jim tried to protect his young cousin from much of the hazing, but could not affect tradition that allowed rabbits to be regularly thrown up against walls and shoved at will by upperclassmen. During rough times, Bob Jr. would glare at his cousin and say, "Anderson, what have you done to me by talking me into coming to school here?"[31]

However, Bob Jr. and Jim were more than blood kin—they were close friends. In fact, Jim was an only child and considered Bob Jr. to be like a brother. They spent free time at the home of Jim's mother, Mildred Anderson, who had moved to Roswell to be near her son.

One semester, Mildred promised Jim she would buy him the automobile of his choice if he made a 98 average in class work. He did, and began driving a cherry red Buick convertible, certainly the hottest car in Roswell.32

The relationship with his cousin paid huge dividends for Bob Jr. after Jim graduated from NMMI and joined the Army. While Jim was in training, Bob Jr. drove the cherry red Buick around town and attracted a small flock of pretty girls. When Jim was home on leave, he drove his car into downtown Roswell. He stopped at a red light and heard a pretty girl say, "Who is that driving Bobby's car?"

Bob Jr. developed good study habits at the military school. He had no choice. Cadets were required to spend two hours each week night at their desks, with a book in hand. "They couldn't make you read it," Jim Anderson said, "but if you had to sit there with it, you usually ended up reading the book."33

Bob Jr. also learned to appreciate history while in high school. He had an incredible ancient history professor, J.H. Kost, lovingly called "Captain Kost," who made history come alive from pages of the textbook. Many years later, Bob Jr. endowed a chair in Kost's honor at NMMI.

While attending NMMI, Bob Jr. became a cadet in the Reserved Officers Training Corps (ROTC) and received artillery training at the school. When he graduated in 1944, World War II was still raging in the Pacific, and he was subject to the military draft. To do his part in the war effort, Bob Jr. landed a spot in the United States Merchant Marine.34

America's Merchant Marine had a gloried past. In the Revolutionary War, without a Navy, the young United States turned to experienced merchant seamen in privately-owned boats and ships to protect its shores against England. Bob Jr. spent nearly three years as a crew member on a number of Merchant

Marine vessels to deliver cargoes and war munitions necessary for American servicemen to carry on the remaining months of the battle for freedom. He made $150 a month, with higher pay when his ship traveled into war zones.

When he could gain shore leave from the Merchant Marine, Bob Jr. still spent holidays at home, which had become the Oklahoma governor's mansion after his father was elected governor in 1942. One Thanksgiving, Grayce set an empty chair at the formal table at the governor's mansion in memory of Bob Jr.'s absence. Bob Jr. also spent several days on leave each summer at the family compound in Minnesota.

As he became a young man, Bob Jr.'s ever-busy father deputized him to train the younger Kerr siblings in the arts of fishing and hunting and to appreciate the football heritage of the University of Oklahoma Sooners.[35]

Bob Jr. and Breene were very protective of their younger sister, Kay. She remembered, "They followed in the footsteps of our father who was very courteous and protective toward women."[36] Bob Jr. felt a special responsibility as Kay's oldest brother. She said, "Even when I was very young, I knew that he was a very generous person, loyal to family and friends, and sensitive to the needs of people around him."[37] While Bob Jr. and Breene were protecting their sister, she was protecting her younger brother, Bill, from the two older boys.[38]

The Kerr boys liked having a little sister around—they even occasionally allowed her into their room at the end of the hall to listen to radio programs after school and put the finishing touches on airplanes made of balsa wood. All the Kerr children loved a string of family dogs. Kay said, "In all our growing up years, dogs were a big part of our lives."[39]

In his teenage years, Bob Jr. was fascinated with guns and history. His grandfather had given him a hunting rifle and taught him how to shoot at targets set up on the Kerr homestead in Ada. Bob Jr. also admired British Prime Minister Winston Churchill, whom he quoted for the remainder of his life.

As his political and business lives consumed more hours each day, RSK was often away from the family. But when he was present, he was always ready to give Bob Jr. and his other children his views on life. Kay remembered, "When our dad was with us, he was really with us, we really connected."[40]

RSK had been impressed with his father's determination to succeed, pointing out that John D. Rockefeller had been successful because he had the ability to associate with men of far greater ability and to establish a community of interest with them. It was RSK's formula for success—knowing great people who could achieve success for themselves while they were contributing to his success. RSK once told Bob Jr., "Boys, be careful what you start. You might succeed."[41]

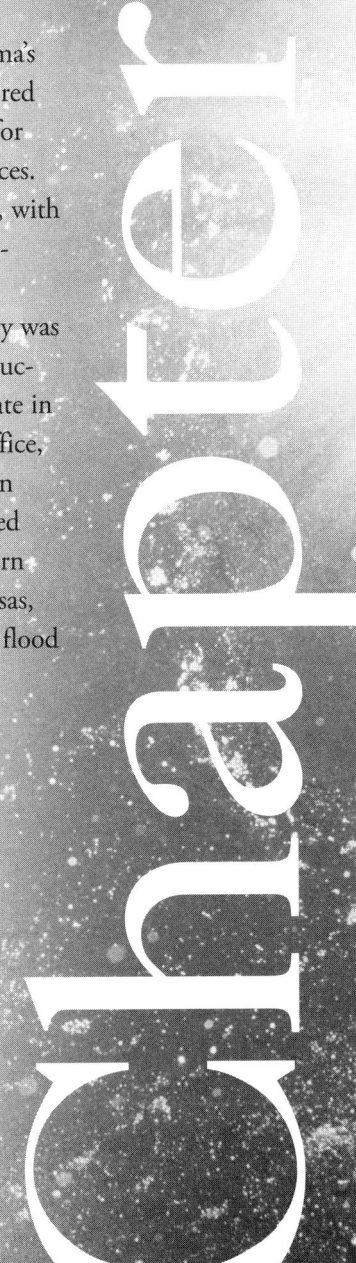

LAND, WOOD, AND WATER

Bob Jr's. legacy of being Oklahoma's "Mr. Water" may have been inspired by observing his father's passion for conserving and harnessing natural resources. Bob Jr. was only 17 years old when RSK, with his booming voice, ready smile, and commanding presence, was elected governor.

Bob Jr. was a bright student and surely was aware of his father's response to the destructive floods that devastated the Sooner State in 1943. Only a few months after taking office, RSK traveled to Muskogee, Oklahoma, in May, 1943 to assess the devastation caused by several days of torrential rains in eastern Oklahoma. Three great rivers, the Arkansas, Verdigris, and Grand, rapidly rose above flood level and consumed everything in sight.

> *It is in our power, under the watchful eyes of God, to determine the physical form of the world in which we live. We can make it a paradise of "land, wood, and water," or by neglect, permit it to become a desert. The choice is ours.*
>
> —Robert S. Kerr

Governor Kerr described the aftermath of the flood, "There were desolate scenes all along the route of the swollen Arkansas—crops under water, rescue boats searching for marooned families, frightened farm animals huddled on high ground, streets awash, and small bridges torn loose, debris frothing and bobbing in the river."[1]

The governor was greatly affected by the suffering of the flood victims. A woman with a baby rose from a crowd of victims and said, "Governor, this is all I have left. I don't know what to do." Another farmer who had seen his English pea crop covered by six feet of water, said, "I watched my life's work disappear before my eyes."[2]

ABOVE: Robert S. Kerr is congratulated by the "Kerr girls" on his election as governor in 1942. Left to right, Kay Kerr, Grayce Kerr, Geraldine Kerr, Maggie Kerr, and Jewell Kerr. *Courtesy Oklahoma Publishing Company.*

LEFT: Bob Jr.'s three siblings, left to right, Kay, Bill, and Breene, try out the Octopus ride at the Oklahoma State Fair. *Courtesy Oklahoma Publishing Company.*

54 MR. WATER: ROBERT S. KERR, JR.

The wave of human misery brought flood control to the forefront of Governor Kerr's agenda to appeal for comprehensive development of the region's river basins. Even though he was governor of only one state, he recognized that flood control was more than a state problem because rivers did not stop at state boundaries.

As governor, RSK faced an almost impossible task of relief and repair of flood-ravaged areas in eastern Oklahoma. In his book, *Land, Wood and Water,* he wrote, "I began to set my sights on a remedial program. This would control the water to prevent the terrible destruction of flood, and to conserve and use it, to lessen and mitigate the damage from drought."3

RSK's involvement after the 1943 Oklahoma floods played a major role in his adoption of the campaign slogan, "land, wood, and water" when he successfully ran for the United States Senate in 1948 and began a legendary career as a champion of river basin development in America.

Bob Jr. listened intently when his father spoke of water as one of the miracles of the universe. RSK said, "Water still excites scientists by its amazing beauty. It allows man to exist on earth…Water covers 70 percent of the earth's surface. It abounds in underground reservoirs and streams. It is hidden in the topsoil and seeps constantly through the subsoil. It exists in all plants. Water fills the air around us as invisible vapor, mist, rain, sleet, or snow. There is a never-ending cycle of precipitation and evaporation."4

Even though RSK became personally aware of devastation caused by uncontrolled water in 1943, flooding was not a new problem. As Americans moved westward in the 19th century and began building along the Mississippi River and its tributaries, government officials were plagued with flooding problems. From 1882 to 1926, state and federal governments spent nearly a third of a billion dollars to build

The Kerr children gather around their mother at the piano in the governor's mansion. Left to right, Bill, Kay, Breene, and Bob Jr. *Courtesy Oklahoma Publishing Company.*

levees to control flooding in the lower reaches of the Mississippi River.[5] Then, the Great Flood of 1927 hit.

When the rains stopped and the flooding subsided, 40 percent of America's lowlands were flooded. A yellow sea, from 50 to 150 miles wide, stretched a thousand miles from Missouri to the Gulf of Mexico. Because so much of the country was affected, the federal government became serious about flood control.[6]

Water resources had always been an issue at the federal level. In 1824, Congress authorized the United States Army Corps of Engineers (Corps) to develop, improve, and conserve the nation's water. The Corps traces its history to June, 1775, when General George Washington requested engineers to begin work on defenses for the Battle of Bunker Hill.

A major component of early Corps projects was flood control, especially in the states drained by the Mississippi River. As early as 1832, the first congressional River Act authorized $15,000 for work on the Arkansas River to maintain a channel to the mouth of the Mississippi. In 1917, Congress passed the first flood control legislation in response to widespread flooding in 1912 and 1913. After more flooding during the Great Depression in the 1930s, the Flood Control Act of 1936 extended the Corps' influence over flood control to the entire country. The Corps' Southwestern Division was created, and 211 flood control projects in 31 states were authorized.[7]

The government's charge over flood control was simple—regulate flood flows and prevent major flood damage. The term "flood control" included using lakes, local protection works, or combinations of dams, levees, and channel enlargement to keep America's rivers in their banks. The Corps also had control over river navigation projects.[8]

The Corps, responsible for the construction and operation of all federal river and harbor projects, became a necessary partner for states such as Oklahoma in building upstream dams to prevent downstream flooding. Most of Oklahoma lies within the boundaries of the Tulsa District of the Corps of Engineers, established in 1939, that maintains a professional administrative and technical staff in Tulsa to oversee Corps operations in the state.

Oklahoma has approximately 500 named rivers and creeks, but is dominated by two major river basins. Northern Oklahoma and much of the central part of the state is drained by the Arkansas River. The remainder of the state is in the drainage basin of the Red River. Except for a few rivers in the Ozark Plateau or the Ouachita Mountains in southeast Oklahoma, streams in Oklahoma flow generally to the east. Water leaves the state into Arkansas through four watercourses, the Red, Arkansas, and Little rivers, and Lee Creek. Glover Creek, in McCurtain County, is the last free-flowing stream in the state.[9]

Water is king in Oklahoma. The state's largest groundwater basin, the Ogallala Aquifer in western Oklahoma, contains more than 80 million acre-feet of water, enough to cover the entire state two feet deep. The state has 22 other groundwater formations, although less than half the water is recoverable.

Oklahoma has more man-made lakes than any other state with more than one million surface acres of water and 2,000 more miles of shoreline than the Gulf and Atlantic coasts combined. Today, there are 60 major reservoirs, most of them constructed by the federal government for flood control. However, flood control projects did not take center stage in Oklahoma until decades after statehood.[10]

Humans created many of the conditions that resulted in Oklahoma being hit hard by lowland flooding in the 20th century. Since the dawn of history, most of the state had received adequate rainfall to support life. The wooded hills and grass-covered plains once efficiently held the water until man, with unplanned development, upset the original balance between soils, grasses, forests, and natural drainage. The result was erosion and flooding.

One of the first organized efforts to control the state's rivers was made by the Oklahoma City Chamber of Commerce in 1923 with the appointment of a flood control committee to promote state legislation. The committee was organized after several Oklahoma rivers, the North and South Canadian, the Washita, and the Arkansas, left their banks and flooded one million acres of bottom land and caused $75 million in damage. The North Canadian, the state's longest river, began at Woodward and tore a path of destruction through El Reno, Oklahoma City, and Shawnee, sweeping buildings from their foundations, washing out highway and railroad bridges, and taking the rich layer of top soil from farm land. Hundreds of thousands of acres of wheat and other crops were destroyed. Oklahoma City was isolated for days without railroad, telephone, or telegraph service.[11]

The North Canadian surpassed by three feet any previous high-water mark and destroyed every bridge that crossed it in Canadian County. Thousands of cattle, hogs, and chickens were victims of the inundation. Six people drowned in Chickasha, swept away by the fast-rising, murky waters.[12]

The most monetary damage was inflicted upon Oklahoma City—damage estimates to the city's water works and dam were $1.1 million. The capital city's chamber of commerce called upon its legislators to formulate a bill to allow land owners to form flood control districts to do something about the flooding that was occurring more regularly and with increasing furor as more people built homes and businesses along the banks of Oklahoma's mighty rivers. A bill was passed, allowing affected property owners to form districts that could float bonds to finance projects.[13]

The Oklahoma City Chamber of Commerce committee, headed by prominent Oklahoma City attorney Ernest E. Blake, and containing prestigious members such as historian Joseph B. Thoburn, department store owner John A. Brown, attorney O.A. Cargill, publisher E.K. Gaylord, and geologist, Dr. Charles Gould, commissioned a survey of 18 counties in Oklahoma and Colorado that lay northwest of Oklahoma City in the North Canadian River basin. The Oklahoma City group worked closely with representatives of 25 cities and towns.

The survey found 27 possible basins, ranging from 2,000 to 13,000 acres, that could hold excess water behind earthen dams. The information was passed along to farmers who began to get serious about forming flood control districts.[14]

Blake wrote in *Harlow's Weekly,* "Oklahoma has an abundance of rivers—more than most areas of similar size. It has an abundance of water, but not an overabundance. Its water falls at inopportune times. It is mostly wasted. It has more than twice as much water as California…yet California is rich in its products…Why? Because they had so little water, they had to conserve it, use it, and profit by it, or perish. We have had just enough to starve through on, and have been too lazy and heedless to conserve what was in a state of nature, waste."[15]

Within two years of its creation, the plan to allow formation of local flood control districts failed. Farm groups eventually opposed the plan, discovering that issuing bonds was in effect a mortgage on individual property. After *The Farmer-Stockman,* a leading newspaper voice for farmers and ranchers, completed a study of the law, editor Carl Williams called for the financing idea to be "laid on the shelf." Williams expressed the opinion of many who believed the 1924 plan did not adequately protect the homes and land of the farmers who were affected.[16]

The Farmer-Stockman was owned by E.K. Gaylord and the Oklahoma Publishing Company, publisher of the state's largest newspaper, *The Daily Oklahoman,* which pulled its support for the flood control district plan even though both newspapers continued their call for some kind of solution to flood control on Oklahoma's rivers. An editorial in *The Daily Oklahoman* said, "Farmers of the state who have paid an assessment of 5 cents an acre to persons who were to fight for the flood control plans have been duped out of their money."[17]

Joining the opposition to the flood control district plan was Oklahoma Governor Martin E. Trapp who demanded Blake's resignation as chairman of the state Drainage, Reclamation, and Irrigation Commission.[18]

Recognizing that Oklahoma could never harness its rivers alone, Oklahoma leaders joined forces with flood control advocates in Arkansas and Texas. The Oklahoma City Chamber of Commerce, in its monthly newsletter, wrote, "We believe the waters of this state that are now wasted by running off into the Mississippi River should be saved. Under active development, 25 years' use of them will double both the population and taxable wealth of the state." The chamber claimed that water was Oklahoma's greatest item of wealth, surpassing even oil or coal.[19]

After another flood in the Canadian River basin hit land owners hard in 1927, Blake, a former Ohio River steamboat pilot, and the Oklahoma City Chamber of Commerce turned to Congress for help. Blake spent four weeks in Washington, D.C., testifying before congressional committees and capitalizing on every opportunity to educate congressmen and senators on how much America needed additional public works projects to control flooding. The idea was to store water upstream in tributaries to prevent flooding the Lower Mississippi Valley. Blake boldly presented maps that explained his mission and charged that flooding of the Arkansas River no doubt caused the catastrophic break of a dike at Greenville, Mississippi, in 1927.

Blake also outlined to Congress a novel concept—an all-purpose reservoir, one which could be used for flood control, irrigation, fish and game, recreation, municipal water supply, and electric power.

Blake's trip did not result in immediate funding from Congress. However, the seed was planted. Congress in 1928 authorized the Corps to make a detailed study of major rivers that eventually emptied into the Mississippi River.

Oklahoma sponsored a flood control conference in Oklahoma City in late 1927 to regionally address the problem. Representatives from Colorado, Texas, Kansas, New Mexico, Oklahoma, Arkansas,

Mississippi, Louisiana, and Alabama attended the conference which was closely observed by members of Congress who were working for long range solutions to flood control.

One organization that grew out of the multi-state meeting was a formal interstate compact with representatives from Oklahoma, Arkansas, Texas, and New Mexico. Ernest E. Blake, Thomas C. Harrill of Gate, and George Kenneck of Wagoner were original Oklahoma members of the compact that was formed for the sole purpose of controlling the waters flowing from the Canadian River system, from its starting point in New Mexico, through Texas and Oklahoma.

Another interstate organization soon created was the Red River and Arkansas Conservation Association, first headed by Ernest E. Blake and Ed Overholser, who was succeeded in 1928 by oil man Frank Buttram. All three men were from Oklahoma City. As its part to fund the effort in the nation's capital to convince Congress to establish a national flood control policy, Oklahoma City paid the association $5,000. Buttram believed that flooding along the Mississippi River would never be corrected until its tributaries, such as the North Canadian and Arkansas rivers, were harnessed by flood control dams.[20]

The Oklahoma City Chamber of Commerce, with Ed Overholser as president and Stanley Draper as manager, led the way in presenting a comprehensive report called "Mississippi Flood Control." In the report, Congress was urged to drop its policy that allowed local communities and states to address flood control alone, citing local control as the culprit that had cost inundated property owners a half billion dollars in 1927. The report clearly accused the federal government of looking out only for the lower Mississippi Valley and neglecting citizens of other states where upstream flooding was becoming an annual occurrence.[21]

The possibility of water transfer was an early political problem that arose during discussions of flood control and water usage in Oklahoma. When rumors surfaced in 1927 that Oklahoma City wanted to transfer water from other rivers for its use, Chamber of Commerce manager Stanley Draper said, "The Chamber of Commerce is not now interested and never has been interested in any plan that contemplated the diversion of water from one river to another in the state of Oklahoma or anywhere else." The clear statement was contained in a letter to the secretary of the Guthrie Chamber of Commerce.[22]

As early as 1891, the idea of harnessing the water of the Grand River in northeast Oklahoma was entertained, and in 1935, the state legislature created the Grand River Dam Authority. The national Public Works Administration (PWA) funded completion of the Pensacola Dam which created Grand Lake. When the Tulsa District of the Corps of Engineers was created in 1939, it received $11 million to complete the Great Salt Plains and Fort Supply lakes already under construction and to design Canton, Optima, and Hulah lakes, and continue oversight of work on Grand Lake, Markham Ferry, and Fort Gibson dams.[23]

Meanwhile, state government had demonstrated only a token, scatter-gun approach to flood control and water conservation. There was always interest in water. The oldest right for the use of stream water still valid was issued to a farmer near Boise City in 1899 by the territorial government. The oldest right for the use of groundwater was issued to the city of Norman in 1894.

The state engineer was responsible for water and irrigation rights and streamflow regulation after statehood. In the 1920s, the Oklahoma Conservation Commission was created to deal with expanding water issues. In 1935, the Planning and Resources Board was authorized by the state legislature to oversee parks, forestry, and water resources. Lake Murray near Ardmore was a project of the state and federal governments. Lake Carl Blackwell near Stillwater was built as a project of the Soil Conservation Service.

A devastating flood along the Red River in 1935 brought congressional authorization for Lake Texoma, completed a year after RSK became governor. At the time, Denison Dam, that backed up water at the confluence of the Red and Washita rivers, was one of the largest dams in the world. As RSK said, "Lake Texoma was born of suffering. The Red River in seven raging floods beginning in 1843 all but drowned the border town of Denison, Texas, as well as the bottom-lands."[24]

Under Governor Kerr, Oklahoma spearheaded the drive for upstream flood control and soil conservation. RSK described himself as a missionary for the idea of farmers building small upstream basins. In fact, 50,000 such reservoirs were constructed during his four years in the governor's office.[25]

RSK's influence was profound. He set in motion an enormous program of water development for the 1950s and 1960s. In the first four years of the 1950s, the Corps of Engineers built four major reservoirs in Oklahoma—Heyburn, Hulah, Tenkiller, and Fort Gibson.[26]

LEARNING THE ROPES

Chapter 4

BOB JR. COMPLETED his military service in the Merchant Marine and enrolled at the University of Oklahoma in the fall of 1947. Upon advice of his cousin, Jim Anderson, Bob Jr. became a member of the Phi Delta Theta fraternity. He married Marilyn LaMoyne Cody, an OU Alpha Chi Omega, on January 23, 1949, at the McFarlin Memorial Methodist Church in Norman. Her father, Reverend Harvey Cody, was a Methodist minister in Miami, Oklahoma. Bob Jr.'s brother, Breene, was his best man.

The following year, Robert Samuel Kerr, III, hereafter referred to as RSK III, was born in Oklahoma City on October 12. Four other children were born in the next 12

> Dad cut a mighty swath in political circles. I learned much from just being at his side, especially when he was trying to convince others to vote with him for a project that benefited Oklahoma.
> —ROBERT S. KERR, JR.

years—Sharon LaMoyne "Shari" Kerr, March 14, 1954; Cody Travis Kerr, May 31, 1955; William Rogers "Billy" Kerr, April 18, 1956; and Valerie Kay Kerr, March 4, 1962.

On the day Shari was born in 1954, her grandfather, RSK, was announcing his candidacy for reelection to the United States

Senate. RSK wrote in a campaign press release, "I got so excited about her advent into the world, I almost forgot about my own debut in the campaign."[1]

Bob Jr., LaMoyne, and RSK III lived in Norman until Bob Jr. graduated from OU with a bachelor's degree in May, 1951. Three months later, after receiving artillery training at Fort Sill, Oklahoma, he and his brother Breene were both called to active duty as America's involvement in the Korean Conflict escalated. While Bob Jr. was overseas, LaMoyne and RSK III lived with her parents in Durant where Reverend Cody had been assigned as pastor of the First Methodist Church.[2]

The wedding party at Bob Jr. and LaMoyne's wedding in 1949. Left to right, front row, Harvey Cody, called "Pampere" by grandson Robert S. Kerr III, Thelma Cody, LaMoyne, Jackie Jones, Bob Jr., Grayce Kerr, and Robert S. Kerr. Back row, James K. Anderson, Jacquie Cody, Harvey Cody, Jr., Kay Kerr, Bill Kerr, Maureen Maze, and Breene Kerr.

In the spring of 1953, Bob Jr. completed his active military duty and moved his family to a small two-story house on Northwest 40th Street in the Crown Heights section of Oklahoma City. Later, they moved just a block to a house on Northwest 39th Street. Bob Jr. he enrolled in the OU School of Law in Norman, where he graduated in 1955. After law school Bob Jr. and a group of Oklahoma law students whose studies had been interrupted by war service successfully petitioned the Oklahoma Supreme Court to waive the taking of the bar examination.

Bob Jr. was a serious student in law school. Classmate William "Bill" Ross said, "He really had a passion for the law. He took his studies to heart. He was personable and the professors liked him."[3]

Bob Jr. had been guided toward practicing law by his father who believed lawyers were members of a special calling. RSK thought it was a special privilege to be able to enter a courtroom and help an underdog against a better financed opponent.

Bob Jr. also continued his military service as a civilian. He was promoted to captain in the United States Army Reserve, serving in the headquarters unit, 95th Division Artillery, until 1957.

Bob Jr. began private law practice in the fall of 1955 in Oklahoma City. He handled commercial, oil and gas, real estate, and banking law cases, but preferred talking with city and state leaders about water development. As a young lawyer, Bob Jr. began formulating ways he could bring about judicious development of Oklahoma's water resources. He believed his father's theory that man's progress can be measured by his use of waterways. He recognized that prehistoric man had been drawn to the rivers by hunger and curiosity and that towns and villages most often sprang up in Oklahoma and other spots on the frontier along

Bob Jr. was a captain in the United States Army artillery in Japan during the Korean War. He served until 1953.

In 1959, the Kerrs moved to a much larger house on Huntington Avenue in Nichols Hills, a suburb of Oklahoma City. LaMoyne and her friends experimented with all kinds of recipes using tuna. The result of the experimentation was a tuna salad that continues to be a family favorite. Left to right, Shari Kerr, Billy Kerr, Cody Kerr, RSK III, LaMoyne, and Bob.

LEFT: Robert S. Kerr, III, is his father and grandfather's namesake. He was born in 1950 and remembered his parents as strict disciplinarians. Disrespect for any one was not excused or accepted. RSK III shared an interest in guns with his father.

ABOVE: RSK III and Shari Kerr. Shari, later in life the Kerr child who looks most like her father, recalled that her parents would not tolerate bad language. Any Kerr child who cursed or repeated slang words had their mouths washed out with soap. Their parents would not tolerate racist terms or any words that were derogatory to anyone else.

rivers and streams. Water was indispensable in sustaining life for humans, their crops, and their animals.

One of the first projects that Bob Jr. was involved in was the Arkansas River Navigation Project. Nearly a decade before, in 1946, a comprehensive plan of development for the Arkansas River was authorized by Congress in the Rivers and Harbors Act as a result of several years of uniting advocates of water and soil conservation, hydroelectric power, flood control, and navigation.

ABOVE: Bill and Valerie Kerr.

Much of the push for the plan came from Oklahoma's congressional delegation and the joint efforts of Governor Kerr and Ben T. Laney, governor of Arkansas.

RSK had won the casual approval for the idea from President Franklin D. Roosevelt, whose priority was America's involvement in World War II. However, Harry S. Truman became president after Roosevelt's death and became an avid supporter of the Arkansas River project.

To promote development of the Arkansas River, Congress authorized the Arkansas-Oklahoma Interstate Water Resources Committee, made up of three members from Arkansas and Newton T. "Newt" Graham, Donald O. "Don" McBride, and T. Elmer Harbour from Oklahoma. The committee helped keep the congressional delegation informed and issued an in-depth report

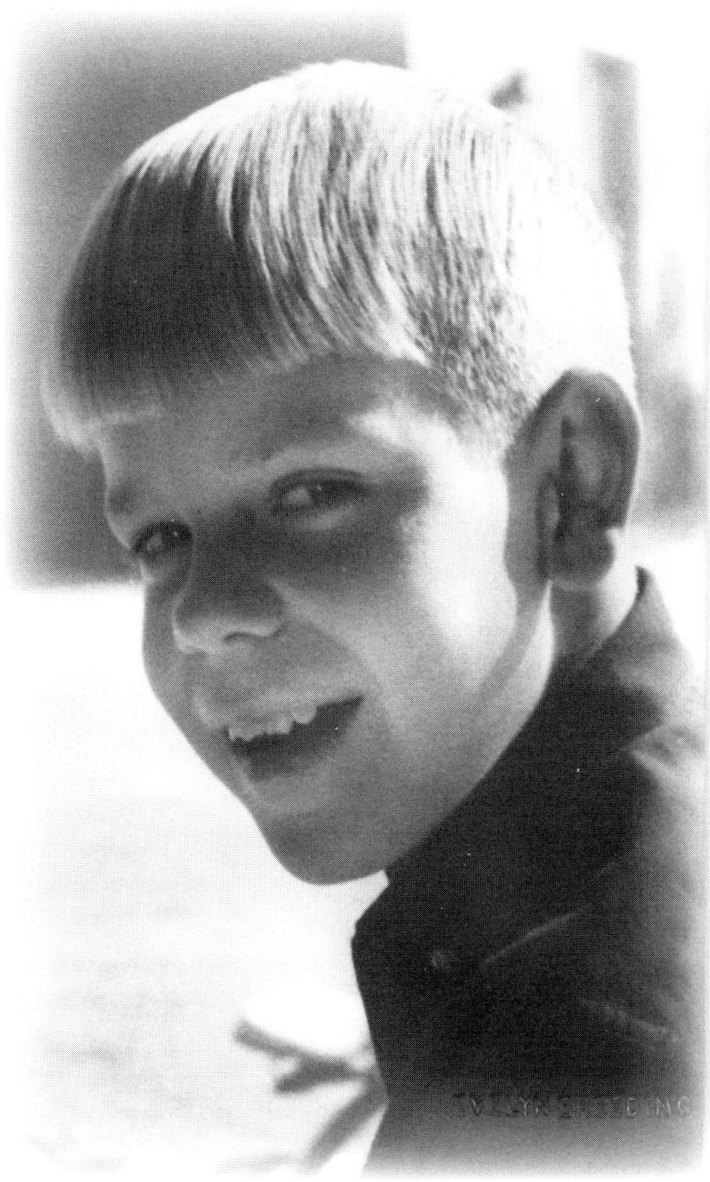

ABOVE: Cody Kerr.

LEFT: Shari and Valerie Kerr.

compiled by the Corps that laid out a workable plan for flood control, irrigation, hydroelectric, and navigation projects on the Arkansas River and its tributaries.

The committee, with Graham, as its chairman, operated as a brain trust for congressional hearings on the plan. The final legislation authorized the Arkansas River Navigation Project, a long range plan that included navigation from Catoosa, Oklahoma, to the Mississippi River. The project was later officially named the McClellan-Kerr Arkansas River Navigation Project for RSK and United States Senator John McClellan of Arkansas, the two statesmen who made it happen.[4]

At the organizational meeting of the Arkansas Basin Development Association in February, 1946, Newt Graham talked about the future, as Congress was realizing the importance of flood control, "Someday it will protect three million acres of rich but flooded valley land, a third of which has been abandoned to woods…Of course, some folk still scoff at navigation, even in the face of favorable findings of engineers after nine years of intensive study."[5]

After RSK was elected to the United States Senate in 1948, work began in earnest on the Arkansas River Navigation Project. His first bill, since called the "Kerr Plan," created a coordinated committee of federal agencies to work with states to study the immense possibilities of river navigation, which was not a new occurrence on the Arkansas River.

In 1800, early French explorers and traders used the river to trade goods to Indians for furs and skins. They used bull-boats, constructed by stretching buffalo hides over a tree-limb framework; pirogues, hollowed-out logs; flatboats, and keelboats to navigate the Arkansas.

In 1819, Colonel A.F. Chouteau built a shipyard in the Three Forks Area where the Verdigris River joined the Arkansas.

Chouteau's boats were up to 80 feet long and carried 50 tons of freight. After Fort Gibson was built in 1824, heavier river traffic brought supplies from New Orleans, Louisiana, Louisville, Kentucky, and other ports. In 1833, 17 boats regularly docked at Fort Gibson.

Oklahoma leaders had long wanted navigation on the Arkansas River. The state's first governor, Charles Haskell, boosted the Arkansas as a navigable stream. In 1908, a steam boat, the "City of Muskogee," carried freight from Fort Smith to Muskogee. The

Robert S. Kerr surrounded himself with experts in water. Left to right, Don McBride, John D. Mayo, General Lewis A. Pick, Kerr, Newton R. Graham, and Colonel Edward G. Daly. *Courtesy Oklahoma Publishing Company.*

Robert S. Kerr poses with his dog, Mr. Ling, on the steps of the United States Capitol in Washington, D.C. Grayce had found the gentle Rotweiler for her husband.

Tulsa Chamber of Commerce began an effort in 1910 by establishing a deep waterways committee to probe the possibility of water traffic on the river. But real progress on making the Arkansas River Navigation Project a reality was never made until Newt Graham, a Tulsa newspaperman turned banker, became interested in navigation.[6]

Graham, dubbed "Admiral of the Arkansas," was convinced that the future of the Arkansas Valley depended on making the river navigable in order to connect eastern Oklahoma to the outside world by inexpensive water transportation of crops and manufactured products. Graham and RSK joined forces with their mutual friend, Don McBride, a professional engineer and state official who had served in two state administrations before RSK became governor.[7]

In 1949, Congress appropriated sufficient construction money to begin the design of what would become the nation's largest civil works project in history except for the space program. Much of the reason was that RSK won a seat on the powerful Senate Public Works Committee because of his involvement as governor in regional natural resources conservation issues.

Republican Dwight D. Eisenhower was elected president in 1952 and was not as enthralled with the Arkansas River Navigation Project as his predecessor, President Truman. In 1952, the project was officially placed in a "deferred for further study" category by the Corps of Engineers. Supporting the delay in construction was the Corps' concern that 100 million tons of silt flowing down the Arkansas each year would surely hinder navigation of the river.[8]

Bob Jr. helped his father develop a three-year strategy to convince Congress and the Corps to begin construction on the Arkansas River Navigation Project in 1957, nearly 40 years after the last steam boats had navigated the Arkansas River from Fort Smith to Muskogee.

RSK's dream was for navigation in both eastern and central Oklahoma, but the Arkansas River was the logical starting point. RSK was intrigued with the mighty Arkansas. He poetically described the river from its starting point at 11,500 feet in the Tennessee Pass on the eastern slope of the Continental Divide, "Snow melting under the sun's hot rays trickles into a crevice small enough to step across…Here at its source, instead of the muddy floodwaters that lap over farms in eastern Oklahoma, is a cool liquid, clear as a diamond."9

Bob Jr. and his Nichols Hills Rattlesnakes baseball team in 1960.

Early proposals for river navigation in Oklahoma met stiff resistance. *The Daily Oklahoman* ran cartoons of RSK in an admiral's uniform, standing on the deck of a boat which was hopelessly stuck in the sandbars of the Canadian River. Undeterred, the Kerrs believed navigation was the key to full expansion of central Oklahoma.10

Don McBride was a key player in producing technical information that would spur water development in Oklahoma. He began as a young engineer hired to improve the waterworks for the city of Carnegie, Oklahoma. One of his problems was the flooding of the Washita River, so McBride began traveling the countryside looking for sites for upstream dams that would hold flood waters for use in times of drought.

RSK, and later, Bob Jr., learned much about "this water problem" from McBride, who had been frustrated in his efforts by the lack of a coordinated front upon which to fight for water development, especially navigation. The Corps of Engineers' authority had been limited for a century to flood control and irrigation.

The Federal Power Commission was in charge of hydroelectric power facilities, the Soil Conservation Service of the United States Department of Agriculture oversaw construction of small dams to prevent erosion, the United States Public Health Service was responsible for eliminating pollution in municipal and industrial water supplies, and the Bureau of Reclamation was crisscrossing Oklahoma building ponds and city water reservoirs.

McBride, a self-described "water rat," was so indispensable in advising RSK on water development, he was sometimes called the "third Senator from Oklahoma." His experience in water development was recognized nationally and was rewarded with a term as manager of the National Reclamation Association. McBride was later director of the Tennessee Valley Authority.[11]

The federal government was not alone in using a less-than-focused approach to water development. In Oklahoma, until the early 1950s, several state agencies, including the Oklahoma Conservation Commission and the Planning and Resources Board, had some responsibility for controlling water. In 1955, House Joint Resolution 520 was passed by the legislature to create the Governor's Water Study Committee made up of legislators and citizens to look at the future.

The committee, appointed by Governor Raymond Gary and chaired by Dr. Lloyd E. Church of Wilburton, surveyed Oklahoma's water problems and recommended a separate state agency be created to administer water rights and deal with the federal government to make certain Oklahoma's water resources were used efficiently.

In 1957, the legislature agreed with the water study committee and created the Oklahoma Water Resources Board (OWRB). Its first chairman was Guy H. James of Oklahoma City. Initially, the OWRB was given the job of managing the state's water supplies and developing a long-range plan for water usage and conservation.

For nearly the first decade of its existence, the OWRB was hampered by insufficient funding and a small staff. But federal legislation, through the Water Resources Planning Act of 1965, provided much needed funds to states to prepare water management plans.

Water planners had a major task before them. It was a fact that Oklahoma had an abundance of water, yet the state was water poor because it allowed water to destroy land, crops, livestock, homes, and human lives, instead of intelligently harnessing these waters to prevent the destruction and conserving for irrigation, power, recreation, and navigation.

So much was at stake. Oklahoma had to do a better job of managing its water. In the previous 50 years, one-third of the top soil had been eroded and washed away. RSK said, "The skeleton on which it was once form and body, now stands exposed on Oklahoma hills and uplands in the glare of the Oklahoma sunshine reminding us that if Oklahoma in the future is to be what she is capable of being, a greater program of conservation and rebuilding of the soil must take place."[12]

The valleys of the Arkansas and Red rivers constituted the breadbasket of America, producing most of the nation's winter wheat and offering unlimited opportunities for inexpensive generation of hydroelectric power. It was also apparent to everyone involved that the Arkansas and Red rivers were the only two major streams in the watershed of the Mississippi River where water transportation and navigation had not been exploited.

RSK believed that water transportation would have a positive practical effect upon Oklahoma's economy. He said, "Water transportation to central Oklahoma would increase the price of Oklahoma wheat a minimum of five cents a bushel; of Oklahoma cotton a minimum of one dollar and twenty-five cents a bale, and effect a greater production at a reduced cost by reason of availability of mineral fertilizer at a reasonable cost."[13]

The fledgling OWRB found that Oklahoma had access within its boundaries to more than six times more water than it used annually. But unfortunately, the water was not always in the right place at the right time. The water story was very much a function of the state's inequitable rainfall pattern. In the western end of the Oklahoma Panhandle, farmers were lucky to receive 15 inches of rain annually. However, water users in southeast Oklahoma receive as much as an unmanageable 56 inches a year. It was not uncommon for the same edition of the daily newspaper to report on a debilitating drought in western Oklahoma and devastating floods in another part of the state.

Bob Jr. was honored to introduce his father at a black tie affair in the Persian Room at the Skirvin Hotel in Oklahoma City in June, 1962. The appreciation dinner brought together 600 business, professional, and industrial leaders to pay tribute to RSK. Hosting the event was a committee chaired by publisher

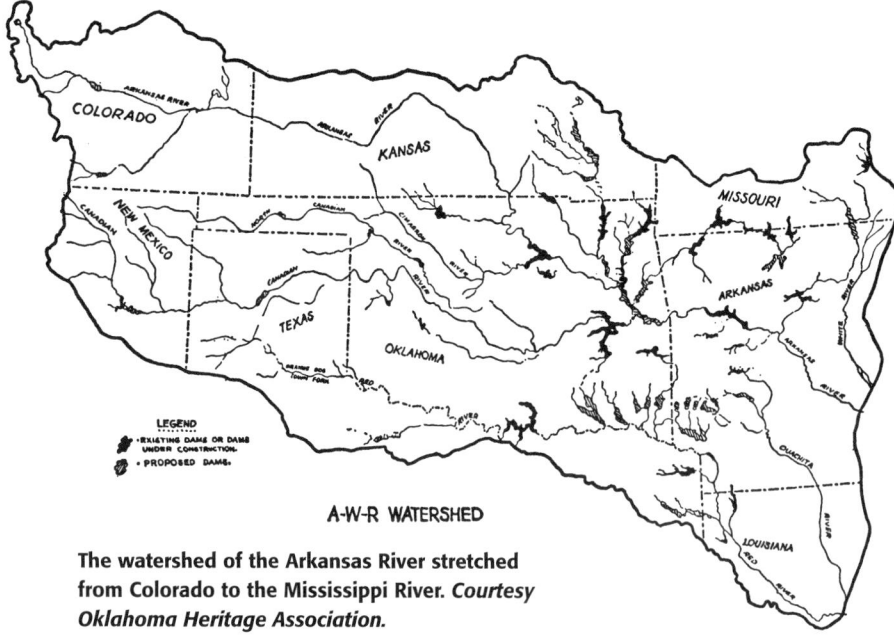

The watershed of the Arkansas River stretched from Colorado to the Mississippi River. *Courtesy Oklahoma Heritage Association.*

E.K. Gaylord and co-chaired by soft drink bottler Virgil Browne, Oklahoma Gas and Electric Company president Donald S. Kennedy, and Roland V. Rodman.[14]

Featured at the RSK appreciation dinner were two of the nation's best known television newsmen, Chet Huntley and Frank McGee. Huntley was half of the Huntley-Brinkley nightly news on NBC, and McGee, a former newsman at WKY-TV in Oklahoma City, was considered one of the premier news reporters at the network level.[15]

After 14 years in the United States Senate, RSK had become one of its most powerful leaders. He was greatly involved in America's space program, especially the race with the Soviet Union to land a man on the moon. There was no question that RSK was the most powerful United States Senator in the arena of water development.

Then, a heart ailment struck RSK, causing his death at age 66 on January 1, 1963, leaving a large vacuum in Oklahoma's leadership. In a rare front page editorial, *The Daily Oklahoman* declared, "Oklahoma's ablest and most honored native son was struck down…in the prime of his power and at the pinnacle of his career."[16]

Vice President Lyndon Johnson, one of RSK's closest friends, said, "America has lost one of our most important resources. He lived well and died well and God will receive him with open arms. He had the strength of the pioneers of old and the daring of the pioneers of today, and gave both to his country in full measure."[17]

Now, whether he liked it or not, at age 36, Bob Jr. was at center stage of the legendary Kerr family and of a series of events in the following weeks that some historians have labeled the most exciting time in Oklahoma history.

Robert S. Kerr built a beautiful family ranch house near Poteau.

CHAPTER 5: BEARING THE BURDEN

As the oldest child, Bob, Jr., hereafter referred to as Bob, was expected to be the Kerr child who had it all together. RSK had grown up as the oldest son and was chided by his father to organize the siblings into a productive force on the Pecan Valley farm. Following that pattern, RSK put a heavy burden upon Bob to be in charge of his siblings when he was away. Bill Kerr observed, "There was no doubt that Dad expected more from Bob because he was the oldest."[1]

With the sudden death of RSK, Bob was suddenly thrust into a new role as the titular head of the Kerr family. His mother was still alive, but looked to Bob for guidance in both personal and business affairs. Within hours of RSK's death, Bob, his brothers, and

> Since Bob was the eldest son, Dad expected more of him. He knew when he was gone, Bob would have to lead the family.
>
> —William G. Kerr

Dean McGee flew in a gleaming new Kerr-McGee turbojet to Washington, D.C.

Even before RSK's funeral, Oklahoma coffee shops and government leaders' conference rooms were buzzing with one question—who would succeed RSK? At the time, the Oklahoma constitution provided that the governor could appoint someone to fill the vacancy. At the time of RSK's death, Governor J. Howard Edmondson was attending a University of Oklahoma football bowl game at the Orange Bowl in Miami, Florida, so Lieutenant Governor George Nigh was acting governor. Nigh, who constitutionally could have immediately filled RSK's position, was a gentleman and waited for Edmondson to return to make the decision.

The day after RSK's death, bold newspaper headlines mourned his loss and speculated who would replace him. Many observers predicted Governor Edmondson, or his brother, Congressman Ed Edmondson, would be appointed to serve two years until the next general election. Bob was also mentioned as a possible replacement.

At first, the governor did not want the appointment, even though many observers assumed he was the logical choice because of his close friendship with President John F. Kennedy. That friendship, political pundits predicted, could mean instant influence for Oklahoma in dealing with the national administration. However, the governor wanted his brother to have the job. Congressman Edmondson said he would take the job only if the Kerr family would agree to support him in a reelection bid two years later. The congressman knew that unless the Kerr organization was behind him, reelection would be an uphill battle in 1964.[2]

President John F. Kennedy, left, and Vice President Lyndon B. Johnson, leave Oklahoma City's First Baptist Church after the funeral of Robert S. Kerr. Later as president, Johnson appointed Bob to the President's Air Quality Advisory Board.

There was no doubt that Bob wanted to succeed his father. For a decade, he had worked with his father on several projects, especially the Arkansas River Navigation Project. Bob had inherited his father's vision of bringing river navigation to central Oklahoma and knew that the success of any such project depended upon Oklahoma having a powerful force in Congress.

President Kennedy joined thousands to honor RSK at his funeral at First Baptist Church in Oklahoma City. Even though RSK's friends were there to honor his life of service, prevalent upon their minds was his replacement in the Senate. As organ music filled the sanctuary of the church, Vice President Johnson leaned toward the president and whispered in his thick and raspy Texas voice, "Please get your friend, Governor Edmondson, to appoint Bob Kerr, Jr." The suggestion was intended to be private between the two top leaders of the United States. However, the sentence was heard clearly by aides sitting nearby.[3]

Leaving RSK's funeral service at First Baptist Church in Oklahoma City, Edmondson turned to Kennedy on the church steps and asked, "Should I appoint Robert S. Kerr Jr.?" Kennedy shrewdly asked the governor, "Would he appoint your son if your positions were reversed?" Edmondson snorted, "Hell, no!" The president chuckled and said, "Then that answers your question, doesn't it?"[4]

Edmondson quickly met with three of RSK's closest lieutenants, Oklahoma House Speaker J.D. McCarty, Rex Hawks, and H.I. Hinds, and Aubrey Kerr, Sr. All agreed that whoever was appointed needed the backing of the Kerr family. Edmondson was still unsure what to do. He offered the job to his brother, but the congressman flatly declined unless and until the Kerr family could enthusiastically support his appointment.

Within a few days, Howard and Ed Edmondson came calling at Bob's home in Nichols Hills to ask if the Kerr family wished the appointment for Grayce Kerr to fill the unexpired term of her late husband. Bob's reply was, "Under no circumstances!"5 Next, the governor suggested that Aubrey Kerr deserved the job for all he had done for his late brother. Bob told the governor that Aubrey could not take the job because of a heart condition.6

The meeting, attended by the Edmondsons and several of RSK's aides, including Burl Hays and Bill Reynolds, took place in Bob's dining room. RSK III was only 12 years old, but remembered the seriousness of the meeting and the fact that the children were ushered out of the room to their upstairs playroom.7

After talking about other possible persons to nominate, the governor looked at Bob, and asked, "Bob, do you want it?" According to Edmondson, Bob rose from his chair and walked to a window. He said nothing for awhile, then turned to the governor and commented, "All I know is I want to work on my father's program, help carry it out. I, uh, just don't know."8

Bob was torn. His mother wanted him to have nothing to do with politics and had contacted Dean McGee to enlist his help in talking Bob out of taking the appointment. Yet Bob wanted to continue his father's public service. There were other considerations. He had a young family and financial obligations. It would difficult to uproot his family and move them to Washington, D.C. He was being asked to make the decision in an emotionally charged atmosphere just days after his father's death. Shari Kerr remembered how her grandfather's death had affected her father, "I was sitting beside the bed when he took the call that grandfather Kerr was dead. Bob began weeping, the first time Shari had seen her father cry."9

Governor Edmondson finally offered the Senate appointment to Bob, but with strings attached. Edmondson wanted Bob to promise that he would only fill out the remaining two years of his father's term, leaving the field wide open for Edmondson and others to pursue the job in the 1964 election.[10]

It was a tempting offer. Even some of Bob's advisors urged him to accept the condition, knowing that he could change his mind and run for reelection. However, Bob would never think of being dishonest and compromising his integrity. He told the governor that he would take the appointment, but only if no strings were attached.[11]

Edmondson told reporters that the Kerr family was really not interested in the appointment. Bob's memory of the meeting with the Edmondsons was different. He told a newspaper reporter, "I talked to the governor for two hours Saturday and made it very clear I wanted the appointment."[12]

In the end, Governor Edmondson, at the end of less than a stunningly popular term, resigned, allowing the new governor, George Nigh, to appoint him to the vacant senatorial position. Before he made the decision public, Edmondson called Breene Kerr and said, "I've made up my mind. I'm taking the Senate job myself. Anything I can do for your family, I will. I'd like to be your friend, keep your dad's people on…" There was no response on the other end of the line.[13]

Nigh served nine days as governor, the first of four different terms as governor of Oklahoma. Edmondson was defeated two years later in his bid for reelection. In fact, he never made it to the general election to face former University of Oklahoma football coach Charles "Bud" Wilkinson, the Republican nominee.

Edmondson was defeated by Lawton State Senator Fred R. Harris who served as United States Senator from Oklahoma for a dozen years and won substantial national support in his bid for the Democratic presidential nomination. Harris, in his book *Potomac Fever,* wrote, "Edmondson resigned and had himself appointed to the Senate. In so doing, he earned the undying enmity of the Kerr family—Grayce Kerr, the senator's widow, and this three sons and a daughter. They felt they had been dealt with cavalierly."14

Bob made clear his feelings about the matter when he announced he "expected" to be a candidate for the United States Senate in 1964. Bob told veteran political writer Otis Sullivant, "If I had to make the decision tomorrow to file for the Senate, there would be no question in my mind. I would file. I would campaign and I would hope to be successful."15

Edmondson's difficult time in being reelected was predicted by Sullivant, "The position of Senator Kerr's eldest son makes it clear the Kerr family and the inner circle of the Kerr forces do not approve of Governor Edmondson succeeding the senator."16

Sullivant, a seasoned observer of Oklahoma politics, recognized the power that Bob would bring to a statewide race, "Kerr hasn't taken much part in politics, although he helped his father at times. He will have be built into a candidate with preparations for a campaign and much groundwork. The name of Robert S. Kerr will be a great vote-getting factor with a candidate of stature and ability to campaign and mix with the voters."17

Sullivant continued, "Kerr will have a tremendous appeal by merely saying he wants to finish his father's work and he thinks a Kerr has the right to it."18

Fred Harris, writing 14 years after RSK's death, analyzed the threat of Bob being a candidate in the 1964 Senate race, "Young Kerr was as tall as his father and looked a great deal like him. He was the beneficiary of the almost automatic support of the Kerr people. But it was already being said that he was no Bob Kerr… young Kerr was shy and did not relish shaking hands with hordes of people and asking for their votes. He'd never liked politics, which he'd regarded as his father's business, not his."19

Harris also wrote, "People soon began to say that young Kerr would never actually file as a candidate for the Senate, that he'd only been pushed into political activity by his mother and the rest of the family."[20] Harris was eventually right about Bob not running for the Senate in 1964, but he had been misinformed about the feelings of Grayce Kerr. In fact, Grayce did not want Bob to run. Bill Kerr recalled, "Our mother didn't think that a political life was necessarily the best situation for Bob. He had a young family, and mother pointedly told him he should not run. She was not passive in that regard."[21]

In the months following his father's death, Bob seriously considered the 1964 race. He hired H.W. "Coach" McNeil, the political coordinator of W.P. "Bill" Atkinson's unsuccessful 1962 race for governor, to survey the landscape and put together a campaign plan. However, in April, 1963, Bob considered his options and announced he would not be a candidate. He told a news conference, "Unexpected developments force me to announce reluctantly that I will not be a candidate for the Democratic nomination for senator in 1964."[22]

Bob cited "increased and unforeseen responsibilities" connected with the administration of his father's estate and his busy law practice as legitimate reasons that would preclude him from "extensive visits and discussions with the citizens of Oklahoma."[23]

After Bob's announcement, Allan Cromley, Washington Bureau chief for *The Daily Oklahoman,* wrote, "The sound you hear, like wind in the trees, is a sigh of relief by Democratic members of the Oklahoma congressional delegation, now that Robert S. Kerr, Jr. has withdrawn from next year's U.S. Senate race."[24] Cromley correctly reported the feelings of Oklahoma Democrats who had dreaded the prospect of being in a campaign crossfire between Bob Kerr's son and the brother of Congressman Ed Edmondson.

With Bob out of the race, Fred Harris was beneficiary of rumors that the Kerr family would bankroll his campaign completely. Harris did not discourage that talk because it helped give him standing as a serious candidate. He later reflected, "And I did get some assistance from them, though not nearly so much as I had hoped for, nor anywhere close to what observers believed I was getting."[25] The Kerr family did pay the salaries of three Harris campaign staff members who had worked for RSK in Washington, D.C.

Grayce Kerr was a vocal supporter of Harris in his successful campaign. She told a newspaper reporter, "Bob told me that Fred Harris had tremendous ability, unquestioned integrity, and was courageous and a dedicated worker…I will vote for Fred Harris because I am convinced that he is the most qualified man to continue and effectuate the program of land, wood, and water."[26]

Marty Hauan, the only man to serve as press secretary to two Oklahoma governors, and the author of several Oklahoma political books, summed up the actions of Edmondson in having himself appointed to the Senate, "Howard got his full taste of the hell which hath no fury like that of a rich woman whose offspring is scorned. He got beat by Fred Harris."[27]

For the remainder of his life, Bob never publicly talked about the 1963 high drama surrounding the appointment of his father's replacement in the United States Senate. It was an example of him seeing the big picture of what was good for Oklahoma and not picking fights over situations that really did not matter in the long run. He became friends with Howard and Ed Edmondson and never held any grudges for their actions.

Chapter 6

LIGHTING A NEW TORCH

RSK left a substantial fortune to his widow and children. The "King of the Senate" died without a will, prompting Bob and Dean McGee to be appointed as co-executors of the estate. Attorney Jack T. Conn explained to Oklahoma County Judge C.J. Blinn that although RSK had scrupulously attended to the business of the public, he "was not equally concerned about his own affairs."[1]

Conn had a long association with RSK. They were law partners, and Conn had introduced RSK at the news conference at which RSK announced for governor in 1942. Conn wrote in his autobiography, "In the years 1960 through 1962, the Senator emphasized the need of preparing a last will and testament acceptable to him and his wife. He

> Although Dad was a serious student of his father's personal success in water development, he recognized that Oklahoma in the 1960s needed to change its water development agenda.
>
> —Robert S. Kerr III

Bob, left, and Dean A. McGee, right, were appointed as co-executors of the Robert S. Kerr estate. In this photograph, they talk with Dr. Paul Keesee, the manager of the Kerr Ranch at Poteau, Oklahoma. *Courtesy Oklahoma Publishing Company.*

asked me to draft a mutual and conjoint will to be considered by him and Grayce…I prepared several drafts. None suited. The principal hang-up was Bob's desire to make sizeable bequests to the Baptist Church, a beneficiary for whom Grayce was less than enthralled."2

Later, while rummaging through a safe deposit box, Bob found a will his father had executed in 1939. Because the will gave his wife less annual income than she was receiving in 1963, the probate court ultimately voided the will and allowed Grayce and the children to inherit under the intestate laws of descent and distribution. 3

Bob took a major role in distributing the assets and forming the Kerr Foundation with the idea of providing a venue to fund programs that could sustain the legacy of RSK. Bob, as the oldest child, also assumed a leadership role in the family and stepped into his father's gigantic shoes in pressing for development of Oklahoma's water resources.

The RSK probate caught the attention of one of the nation's best known newspaper columnists, Drew Pearson. In his syndicated column, Pearson wrote, "Grayce Kerr, the senator's widow, is sitting in the driver's seat…reorganizing the cattle, oil, law, and political fortunes of the Kerr empire."[4]

Bob, asked by another reporter to respond to the Pearson comment, said, "There is no more basis in fact for this article than there is in reporting that Drew Pearson is about to become a mother!"[5] The true story was that Bob and Dean McGee worked closely together with Grayce to manage the affairs of the Kerr estate, which was initially estimated to be valued at $40 million.

Bob became titular head of the law firm of Kerr, Davis, Irvine, Krasnow, Rhodes and Semtner. The firm became counsel to Fidelity Bank, N.A., run by former Kerr lawyer, Conn, and was principal outside counsel to Kerr-McGee Oil Industries. RSK and Dean McGee had become principal shareholders in Fidelity Bank in previous years, and Bob was prominent in the effort to convince Conn to leave Ada in 1964 to become president of the bank.

The Kerr children became closer after their father's death. While RSK was alive, Bob and his brothers and sister had largely gone their own ways, with only occasional family gatherings. But their father's death changed that. The youngest Kerr son, Bill, remembered, "At that point we became friends. We had to develop a higher relationship than just being siblings. We went through a lot of political and business things together."[6]

Bill officed with Bob and learned great respect for his oldest brother. He said, "Bob was gentle, slow to act, but very positive when he did so. He was a great mentor, he had our father's patience, and was a good hearted man."7

Bob and his brothers had learned much from their father. In fact, they could not escape his moments of teaching. There is no doubt that RSK's passion for developing Oklahoma's water came from his father. Bill remembered, "We heard a lot about the importance of water to Oklahoma over and over again. I think maybe Dad was rehearsing some of his raw thoughts in these monologues he would give in a fishing boat, where he had a captive audience. There really isn't any place to go. I'd been surprised if Bob could have avoided having an interest in Oklahoma water."8

Bob took up where his father left off by saying, "Oil is Oklahoma's past—water is Oklahoma's future." That was a startling statement, especially since Bob became an active member of the board of directors of Kerr-McGee Corporation, to represent his family's interest on the governing board of the huge conglomerate of energy related companies.

Bob became increasingly active in civic affairs. In 1963 he was elected vice president of the Oklahoma City Chamber of Commerce, was active in the annual United Way drive, and served on the boards of several more civic and educational organizations. James D. Fellers, president of the Oklahoma Bar Association, appointed Bob as chairman of a statewide committee of lawyers to explore world peace through law.

In July, 1963, Bob was appointed as general chairman of the Freedom Bond drive to encourage purchase of savings bonds in Oklahoma City. In December, 1963, Bob oversaw the relocation of his father's body from a mausoleum in Oklahoma City to a permanent resting place near the log cabin south of Ada where he was born.9

A month after President John F. Kennedy was assassinated in Dallas, Texas, Bob and Dean McGee narrowly escaped death when their airplane spun off the runway at President Lyndon Johnson's ranch airstrip near Johnson City, Texas. The right wheel of the twin-engine Beechcraft collapsed on landing. Witnesses said the aircraft did a partial ground loop but fortunately did not overturn. Bob and McGee shook off the hard landing and attended a barbecue with President Johnson and West German Chancellor Ludwig Erhard.[10]

Bob continued to spend much time in 1964 wrangling with tax and probate lawyers over his father's estate. The lack of estate planning on RSK's part eventually cost the Kerr heirs nearly $10 million in federal estate taxes.

In August, 1964, Grayce Kerr married Tulsa oilman Olney Flynn, the 1946 Republican nominee for governor of Oklahoma. Bob announced the marriage to the press after his mother had confided in him the possibility of marriage the week before. The romance between Flynn and Mrs. Kerr had begun 40 years before, long before they each married someone else. A year after RSK's death, Grayce and Flynn began corresponding and decided to get married in Minneapolis, Minnesota.[11]

Bob hit the campaign trail for Democrats in the 1964 general election. He traveled the state with Congressman Carl Albert and former Governor Raymond Gary to 20 campaign rallies to urge Oklahomans to elect Fred Harris to the Senate and send President Johnson back to the White House. Oklahomans did both. At a September campaign rally in Poteau, Bob and his brother, Bill, took pot shots at Republicans Barry Goldwater and Bud Wilkinson.

In December, 1964, Bob's mother was diagnosed with cancer that was discovered during a gall bladder operation. Her four children were by her bed at her Nichols Hills home in Oklahoma City on March 2, 1965, when she died. Ironically, within two weeks of the death of his mother, Bob was named the advance gifts chairman for the annual fund drive for the Oklahoma County Division of the American Cancer Society.

By early 1965, Oklahoma's political rumor mills had Bob as a definite candidate for governor of Oklahoma in the following year's general election. Oklahoma Democrats were feverish about retaking the governor's mansion after losing it for the first time in history in 1962 to Republican Henry Bellmon. In June, 1965, Bob told political writer Otis Sullivant, "I have had several people talk to me about it and I have definitely decided to check into it." Bob said he would not make an immediate decision, but would "watch developments and see what appears to be the issues," then decide if he wanted to make the race.[12]

Bob's interest in the governor's race created a stir among other candidates. Newspaper accounts indicated he would be a major contender because of the strength of his father's name and the assurance of an adequate campaign fund. However, Sullivant, writing in *The Daily Oklahoman,* said, "Many of Kerr's close friends and relatives do not want him to run. Dopesters point out Kerr forces will be behind Sen. Fred Harris in the senate race and they do not want top candidates in both races. Others say young Kerr is not ready."[13]

The Democrat most affected by Bob keeping himself in the race early in the campaign was Oklahoma City attorney Preston J. Moore who had run third in the Democratic primary in 1962. Moore was counting on most of his support coming from the remnants of the RSK political machine around the state. Moore secretly told supporters that if Bob ran, much of his money and support would dry up.

In September, 1965, Bob eliminated himself from the governor's race, citing increasing personal business obligations and a

Bob, right, unveils the Robert S. Kerr Memorial Award in 1965. The award was given to Oklahoma astronaut Leroy Gordon Cooper when he returned to earth from an eight-day orbit around the earth. With Bob is John Badger, Jr., president of the Altus, Oklahoma chapter of the Air Force Association. *Courtesy Oklahoma Publishing Company.*

new role as executor of his mother's estate. Grayce Kerr Flynn had left a will leaving the bulk of her $16 million estate in trust for her four children.

One of Bob's duties in probating his mother's estate was to sell off the huge Angus cattle herd on the Kermac Ranch near Poteau, Oklahoma. In 1956, RSK had bought land in the Poteau River Valley, established a home there, increased his land holdings to 46,000 acres, and built one of the nation's largest herds of registered Angus cattle. In January, 1966, Bob oversaw the largest registered Angus auction in North America by a single consignee.

LIGHTING A NEW TORCH **103**

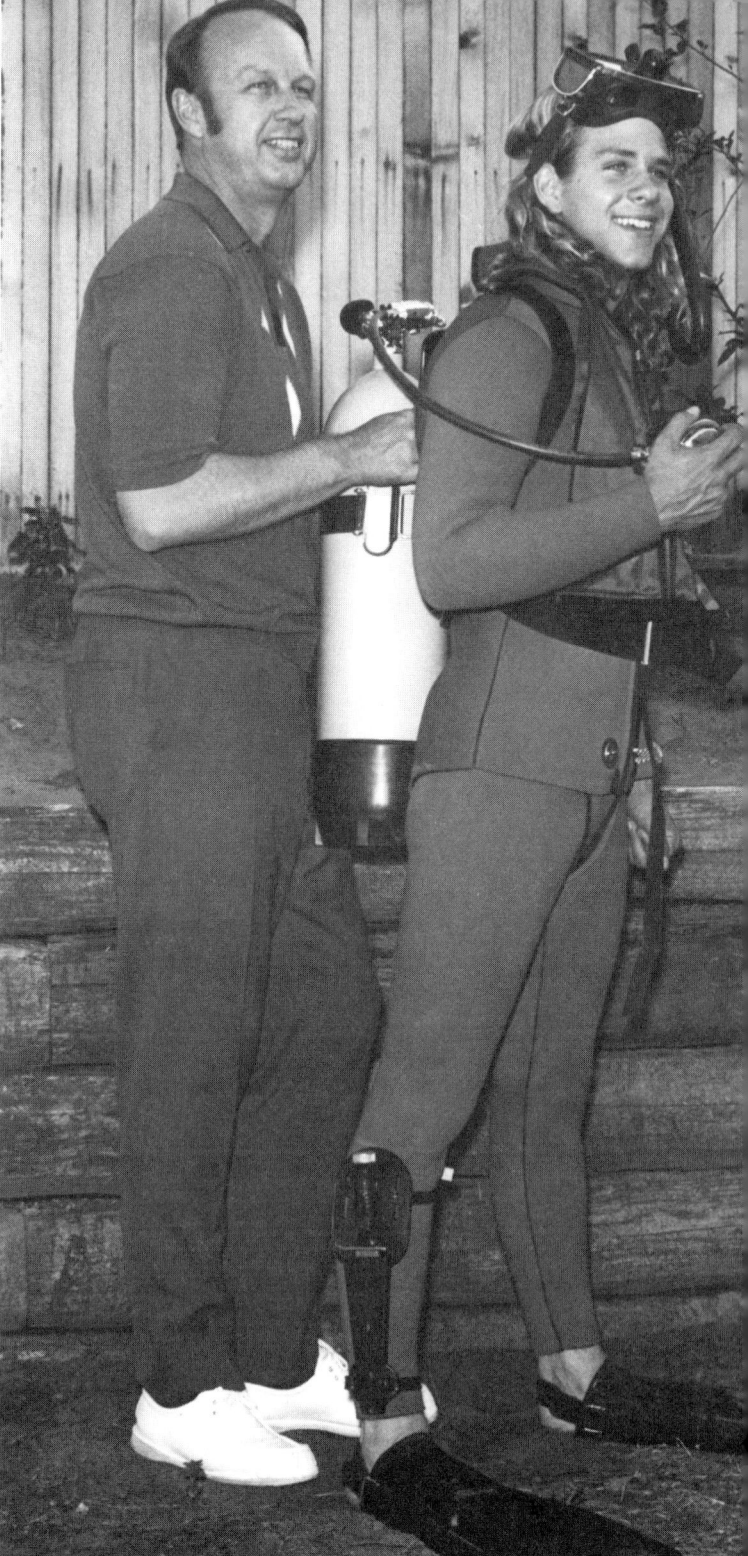

LEFT: Bob, left, and Billy Kerr.

BELOW: Bob was state payroll savings plan chairman in 1966. Left to right, John Morrison, H.A. McNeer, Frank Sewell, George H.C. Green, Bob, and A.E. Bradshaw. *Courtesy Oklahoma Publishing Company.*

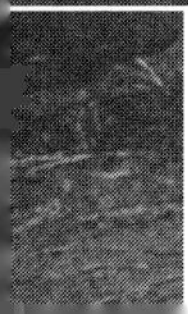

Cattlemen from across the country gathered at the ranch for the auction to bid on the more than 4,000 cattle.[14]

In early 1967, Bob was called as a witness in a federal court trial that made headlines in the nation's capital. Bobby Baker, the legendary secretary to the Democratic majority in the United States Senate, was accused of siphoning huge amounts of cash from contributions he collected for the reelection of Democratic senators. It was an accepted practice for campaign contributions to be made in cash and distributed per a candidate's wishes.

Baker, trying to avoid federal income tax evasion charges, shocked official Washington when he claimed he did not keep $100,000 for himself, but had instead delivered it to Robert S. Kerr a few days before his death.[15]

Edward Bennett Williams, Baker's defense lawyer, told reporters that Baker delivered the money to RSK in three increments, the last being on November 20, 1962, at a three-man breakfast held in the Sheraton-Oklahoma Hotel in Oklahoma City. Williams also declared that RSK handed $35,000 to $40,000 back to Baker as a "loan" and helped Baker obtain a $250,000 line of credit at Fidelity National Bank in Oklahoma City. Williams said RSK had, from his hospital bed shortly before his death, forgiven Baker from repaying the personal loan to "wipe the slate clean" for all the things Baker had done for RSK.[16]

Bob testified that large amounts of cash were found in RSK's safety deposit box, but he had found nothing in his late father's effects to indicate any loan to Baker. Bob had been present at the opening of a safety deposit box at the National Savings and Trust Company in Washington, D.C., when he was searching for his father's will. Bob said he found cash totaling $42,950 in RSK's safety deposit box.[17]

Even though Bobby Baker's defense team tried to drag RSK and Lyndon Johnson into the case, evidence showed that Baker

Bob poses in front of a collection of works by Winston Churchill. Bob often quoted the former British prime minister. *Courtesy Oklahoma Publishing Company.*

Bob reads a statement to the press after testifying at the 1967 trial of Bobby Baker in Washington, D.C. *Courtesy Oklahoma Publishing Company.*

had skimmed large amounts of cash from campaign contributions and then slandered the two men who had given him so much power in the United States Senate.

Baker was convicted of income tax evasion. Some trial observers believed the testimony of Marvin Gaut, president of the Otis Elevator Company, was a turning point for the jury. Gaut was present at the breakfast meeting at the Oklahoma City hotel where Baker alleged he received cash from RSK in the hotel men's room. Gaut testified, however, that neither Baker nor RSK left the table during the meeting. During the trial, Baker conveniently forgot the identity of the third person at the breakfast.[18]

As Bob's interest in the state's political landscape lessened, his youngest brother, Bill, became state Democratic chairman in 1967. Bill was 29 years old and described by political observers as the "natural politician" of RSK's four children.

Bob had been presented the opportunity to leave Oklahoma and partner with his cousin, Jim Anderson, in the oil business in Texas a decade before. Anderson had become successful in drilling for oil in Texas and formally invited Bob to become his partner. However, Bob talked to his father who dissuaded him from leaving his Oklahoma City law firm. To keep Bob from leaving Oklahoma City, RSK gave his oldest son 10,000 shares of Kerr-McGee Industries stock.[19]

Bob was enjoying the fruits of his father's labor in establishing a Kerr tradition of leading the fight to develop natural resources. However, since childhood, he had been intimidated by his father's unprecedented political power, both in Oklahoma and the nation. Bob knew he was living in the shadow of his father—the press always referred to him as "Bob Kerr's son."

Jim Anderson remembered, "He wanted so much to accomplish something on his own. He was never willing to break

110 MR. WATER: ROBERT S. KERR, JR.

The Kerr children at a meeting in the Oval Office at the White House with President Lyndon Johnson. Left to right, Congressman Tom Steed, Kay Kerr Adair, United States Senator Mike Monroney, Bob, Bill, presidential aide James Jones, and President Johnson. The top of Breene Kerr's head can be seen above Senator Monroney. *Courtesy the White House press office.*

A ROBUST ANCESTRY 111

completely with his father, but at the same time he wanted to do something great for Oklahoma in his own name."[20]

Bob desperately wanted to make his own personal mark on Oklahoma's future, and he believed water development was where he could excel.[21]

WATER CHAMPION

IN 1963, the same year of RSK's death, the Oklahoma legislature ordered the Oklahoma Water Resources Board to begin long-range water development studies. Still without sufficient staffing, the OWRB turned to the state's universities and to chambers of commerce to help develop information, although a statewide comprehensive water plan was nearly two decades in coming.

Bob was especially interested in plans to build a United States Public Health Service facility in Ada that would be named after his father. In September, 1964, construction began on the $2.5 million Robert S. Kerr

> *No matter where one lives in Oklahoma, he either has too little or too much water.*
>
> —ROBERT S. KERR, JR.
>
> *Water must not be a partisan subject. It is not a resource for our parties or partisans. The issue of water is action vs. inaction—to win, or not to win.*
>
> —PRESIDENT LYNDON B. JOHNSON

Water Research Center adjacent to the land occupied by the restored cabin in which RSK was born. The research laboratory was established by the federal government to conduct research on water pollution and other water problems.[1]

In 1965, Bob became president of the Water Development Foundation of Oklahoma (WDF), a non-profit group incorporated by his father and others on January 31, 1957, for the stated purpose of "providing a means whereby interested agencies, groups, and individuals could conduct scientific and educational studies and to disseminate the information obtained to the public."[2]

From its inception WDF actively promoted the development of adequate water supplies for central Oklahoma, including the McGee Creek Reservoir, Arcadia Lake, and the Central Oklahoma Project (COP), a long range plan to make the Deep Fork Creek navigable to Oklahoma City.

In 1966, Bob became president of a new Oklahoma non-profit corporation, Oklahoma Water, Incorporated (OWI), which took over the work of the disbanded Oklahoma Reclamation Association.

In announcing the purpose of OWI, Bob said, "The supply of water rarely matches the need. The problem of too little, too much, and too late must be solved. Oklahoma is on the threshold of greatness and an abundance of good water will determine the level of industrial and agricultural achievement for all areas of the state."[3]

The function of OWI was to provide an umbrella under which all organizations concerned with water development in Oklahoma could work together. OWI's purpose was "to sustain life with as much harmony and beauty in the ecological make-up as can be achieved." The organizing documents of OWI recognized that water development was a fiercely divisive issue between western and eastern Oklahoma, politicians, and environmentalists. The new group's motto was, "Oklahoma water for Oklahomans."4

Bob worked closely with Guy N. Keith, manager-engineer of the Water Development Foundation from the early 1960s until he resigned to become a private consultant in 1967. Keith had worked fulltime to seek solutions to central Oklahoma water problems, including the Oklahoma City floodway project and the Central Oklahoma Project.

Keith was replaced by Morrison B. Cunningham, formerly general manager of the Oklahoma Municipal Improvement Authority and superintendent of the Oklahoma City water department. Cunningham was well-known in water development circles, both in Oklahoma and nationally. He was a past president of the American Water Works Association, director of the Water Pollution Control Federation, and past president of the Oklahoma Society of Professional Engineers. He had served on water problem committees under four Oklahoma governors.5

For decades, Oklahoma City leaders had sought an adequate water supply from outside the immediate reaches of the capital city. Bob was on hand in 1967 when the first water from Atoka Lake dumped from the end of a pipeline into Lake Stanley Draper. He said, "This is not a completion, but a beginning. Unless we keep in mind that we are going to need twice as much water 20 years from now as we need today, our children and our children's children won't be able to stay…they'll go where water is, as men always do."6

Oklahoma City Chamber of Commerce President Stanton L. Young echoed Bob's sentiments for expansion of water development projects. As they spoke, construction plans for McGee Creek Reservoir in southeast Oklahoma and Arcadia Lake east of Edmond were being drawn by the Corps of Engineers, and authorization bills were making their way through Congress.

116 MR. WATER: ROBERT S. KERR, JR.

A group of Oklahoma Panhandle leaders interested in water development became key supporters of Bob and Oklahoma Water, Inc. Left to right, State Representative Marvin McKee; Virgil Higgins with the Texas County Irrigation Water Resources Association; attorney Larry Field; State Senator Leon Field; Bryan Wright, Guymon city attorney; H.C. Hitch, Jr. of the Oklahoma Cattleman's Association; Tyrone water commissioner Raymond Mann; and irrigation farmer George Lungrin.

Bob began most of his speeches to civic groups with a central theme, "No matter where you live in Oklahoma, you either have too little or too much water, and it isn't uncommon to see stories in the same edition of the newspaper, reporting devastating flooding in some areas of the state and debilitating drought in others."[7]

Those speeches always preached that each year, an average of 35 million acre-feet of Oklahoma water ran uncontrolled through the state and ultimately to the Gulf of Mexico. An acre-foot of water was one foot of water covering one acre. The surplus water that left Oklahoma's eastern and southern boundaries each year would have covered the entire state with a nine-inch blanket of precious water.[8]

Bob recognized that Oklahoma's real water problem was a water management problem, not a water supply problem. He saw two challenges—develop water in eastern Oklahoma for use in that section of the state and create a plan to redistribute surplus water in eastern Oklahoma to central and western sections of the state.

The controversy about transferring eastern Oklahoma's surplus water had blocked the completion of any comprehensive statewide water plan for years. Scientists and engineers had looked at weather modification, desalination plants, and groundwater development to develop sufficient water for western Oklahoma. However, those exotic approaches had not panned out, and planners always returned to water transfer as providing the answer to Oklahoma's future water needs.[9]

The concept that would be at the forefront of water development discussions in the next three decades was called either water transfer or water conveyance. Whatever the label, it meant catching surplus water when and where it fell and transferring it to holding reservoirs until it was needed in water-hungry sections of the state.

Water transfer was not a new idea. The Babylonians, Egyptians, and Romans built extensive irrigation and water supply systems to meet the demands of their citizens. In the first century, A.D., Roman Emperor Claudius I oversaw the construction of a system of aqueducts to bring water from the mountains into Rome. A thousand years before that, ancient Persians dug underground aqueducts to bring mountain groundwater to arid plains. Much of the irrigation water used in the 1960s in Iran came from that 3,000-year-old water transfer system.[10]

In the 1950s, California constructed a water conveyance system that moved water nearly 700 miles from the high Sierras of northern California to the deserts in the southern part of the state. Bob said, "Oklahoma might well emulate California to the extent that it fits our circumstances."[11]

Bob became the leading proponent of the Central Oklahoma Project, formally known as the Oklahoma Water Conveyance Project, a forward-thinking project that could bring 1.2 billion gallons of pure eastern Oklahoma water to central Oklahoma each day and link Oklahoma City with the Arkansas River Navigation Project that was nearing completion. The plan proposed using Eufaula Reservoir and the Deep Fork Creek to transfer water and barges in a deep channel for 117 miles to Oklahoma City.

 In February, 1967, Bob saw congressional support for the project weakening, especially when it was decided to separate the water canal project from Corps of Engineers' plans to build Arcadia Lake on the Deep Fork Creek. For years, both the reservoir and canal projects were joined together.

Bob was correct in predicting that if the projects were separated, the canal project would be put on the shelf indefinitely and "pose a major threat to Oklahoma efforts to pin down vast amounts of Oklahoma water for Oklahoma use." He said unless the COP was completed, cropland in central and western Oklahoma would never be adequately developed.[12]

Bob served as vice president of the multi-state Arkansas Basin Development Association, Inc., and convinced that group's board of directors in 1968 to back a request to Congress for funds to re-study the navigation features of the COP. The request was made to the public works committees of the United States Senate and the House of Representatives. Congress approved the request and the Corps of Engineers began to reexamine the feasibility of extending navigation to Oklahoma City.

"It is only a matter of time until barge traffic comes all the way to Oklahoma City," Bob told a newspaper reporter. He predicted that Oklahoma's agricultural industry would benefit most by a port in Oklahoma City. At the time, most of the wheat grown in western Oklahoma was being trucked to Houston and New Orleans, a far more expensive way to get grain to market than by river transportation. Oklahoma City Chamber of Commerce manager Paul Strasbaugh said Oklahoma wheat farmers could save $43 million annually by shipping their crops by barge, rather than by rail or truck.[13]

In early 1971, the Corps of Engineers scheduled two public hearings to gather response to the proposed Central Oklahoma Project. The hearings were part of a study to determine the feasibility of connecting Oklahoma City with the Arkansas River Navigation System via Deep Fork Creek and the Eufaula Reservoir. Congress had appropriated $80,000 for the study. The Corps urged representatives from agricultural, commercial, industrial, business, transportation, and utility interests to attend meetings at Fountainhead State Park near Eufaula and East Central State University in Ada.[14]

The idea for extending navigation to Oklahoma City via the Deep Fork died a slow death. In September, 1974, the Corps proclaimed the Central Oklahoma Project economically infeasible. After that death blow, the federal government never again seriously considered the forward-thinking project that could have changed central Oklahoma's economic future.

In February, 1969, Bob formed a new group, the Oklahoma Water Users Association (OWA). He was president, Don Arch King of Guymon was first vice president, Guy N. Keith of Oklahoma City was secretary-treasurer, and Bert Castleberry was executive vice president. The group held its first annual meeting at the Lawtonian Hotel in Lawton, Oklahoma, on September 5, 1969.

Congressman James "Jim" Wright of Texas was the keynote speaker at the OWA meeting. Wright joined Oklahoma Congressman Ed Edmondson in blasting United States Supreme Court Justice William O. Douglas for his attack on the Corps of Engineers in an article in *Playboy* magazine. Douglas accused the Corps of conniving with real estate developers, juggling cost estimates, and rigging economic studies of proposed water resource projects. Douglas called the Arkansas River Navigation Project a "worthless canal."[15]

Bob tapped the leading water advocates in the state for membership on the executive committee of OWA. Members were Joe Tilly of Norman, Frank Taylor and Ben Petitt of Oklahoma City, Mike Wharton and Dick Dillon of Okmulgee, Dr. John Wright of Wagoner, Dr. Lloyd Church of Wilburton, Ted Savage of Ada, Orville Saunders of Altus, Jess Stratton of Clinton, and Frank Raab of Canton.[16]

Bob recognized that any water users group needed the cooperation of state government. OWA's advisory committee was filled with important state government officials such as Myron DeGreer, Norman Flaigg, Forrest Nelson, Jack Odell, Loyd Pummill, Courtney Tidwell, Farrell Copelin, and Spuds Widener.[17]

The founding of OWA received favorable mention in the press. The *Capitol Hill Beacon* in Oklahoma City editorialized, "With his family name and fortune, Bob Kerr could probably play whatever role he wanted to in Oklahoma affairs, but he has chosen to become president of OWA. The association is dedicated to making water run uphill—but for a purpose. It has one aim: to provide all sections of the state with good, clean, usable water."[18]

By the end of 1969, Bob was able to convince several major Oklahoma companies and prominent leaders to financially support the OWA. In the October, 1969, monthly OWA newsletter, it was noted that contributions had been received from architects Benham-Blair and Affiliates of Oklahoma City; the Cotton Electric Coop in Walters; Dierks Forests, Inc., of Broken Bow; Swift and Company and Henry Hitch Farms of Guymon; First State Bank of Gould; and Southwestern Stationery and Bank Supply in Oklahoma City.[19]

Individual contributors to OWA included Seminole publisher Milt Phillips, State Representative Howard Cotner of Altus, former Governor Henry Bellmon of Red Rock, Dr. Bernice Crockett of Durant, banker Phil Symcox of Norman, Judge Burton Duncan of Antlers, lawyer Joe Stamper of Antlers, Congressman Ed Edmondson of Muskogee, and clothier S.K. McCall of Norman.[20]

In 1970, OWA merged its staff and offices with Oklahoma Water, Inc., in an effort to reduce duplication of efforts and increase efficiency of both groups. OWA officially changed its corporate, non-profit name to Oklahoma Water, Inc. New officers were vice president, Dr. Otho Whiteneck, a dentist from Enid, who was president of the State Board of Health, and secretary-treasurer, George Hill, publisher of the *Coalgate Record/Register*.[21]

Bob, left, is greeted at the Guymon airport in 1969 by R.P. Duke, president of the Guymon Chamber of Commerce. Bob was in Guymon to speak on the need for a statewide water plan.

RIGHT: Bob, left, visits with Oklahoma Congressman Tom Steed at an annual meeting of the Oklahoma Water Users Association.

BELOW: Left to right, Bob, Dr. Lloyd Church of Wilburton, and Dr. John Wright of Wagoner discuss the merits of transferring water from eastern to western Oklahoma.

OWI did not leave women out of their efforts to develop Oklahoma's water resources. In 1971, OWI honored four women for their work in water development. Frances Fern Kinkade, president of the Business and Professional Womens Clubs of Oklahoma, was the first woman to serve on Shawnee's city commission. Dr. Bernice Crockett, chairman of Oklahoma Water's Council on Education, conducted water development workshops. She was previously chairman of the Department of Health Education at Southeastern State College in Durant. The other women honored were Dorothy Howell of Haywood and Lois

Norman of Mangum, chairwomen of ladies' events at the OWI 1971 annual meeting in McAlester.22

While water development occupied much of Bob's time, he continued as an active partner in the law firm of Kerr, Davis, Irvine, Krasnow, Rhodes & Semtner, as a director of Kerr-McGee Corporation, and was on the board of directors of Fidelity Bank, N.A. He also was president of Kerr Aviation, based at Wiley Post

Airport in Oklahoma City. The company was the Beechcraft airplane dealer in central Oklahoma and owned storage space for 140 aircraft in two large hangars and 72 individual hangars.

The Kerr Foundation also took a great deal of Bob's time. Breene Kerr served as chairman, and Bob was president of the foundation that funded many worthwhile projects. One of the foundation's principal activities was agricultural research and farm consultation and management programs. The foundation operated a 4,000-acre ranch near Poteau, where agriculture, livestock, fish, wildlife, and forestry projects were conducted by a

team of experts headed by Dr. Roy A. Chessmore.[23]

Bob, left, presides at the first board of directors meeting of the Oklahoma Water Users Association.

In the late 1960s, Bob and OWI monitored the completion of the Arkansas River Navigation Project. In August, 1968, all four of RSK's children were present when ground was broken for a $1.2 million marine terminal near Sallisaw, adjacent to the $92.5 million Robert S. Kerr Lock and

Dam. The Sallisaw facility was built to house the main United States Coast Guard station along the Arkansas River. United States Senators Mike Monroney and Fred Harris, Congressmen Ed Edmondson and Carl Albert, Coast Guard Rear Admiral Russell R. Waesche, and Colonel Vernon W. Pinkey, commander of the Tulsa District of the Corps of Engineers, lauded the efforts of RSK in dreaming of the Arkansas River Navigation Project.[24]

Navigation reached Little Rock, Arkansas, in December, 1968; Fort Smith, Arkansas, in December, 1969; and Catoosa, Oklahoma, in December, 1970. The completion of the project was a milestone in American water projects and brought a new era of industrialization to landlocked Oklahoma.

The McClellan-Kerr Arkansas River Navigation System provided a nine-foot deep channel with a total lift of 420 feet, 448 miles long, from the Mississippi River to the Port of Catoosa near Tulsa, connecting Oklahoma to the Mississippi, Ohio, Missouri, Illinois, Cumberland, and Tennessee rivers and the Gulf of Mexico and the Great Lakes. Seventeen locks and dams, 12 in Arkansas and 5 in Oklahoma, were needed to create the stairway of water. All locks were the same size, 110 feet wide and 600 feet long, the length of two football fields.[25]

The Kerr Foundation published a comprehensive study on the impact of the McClellan-Kerr Arkansas River Navigation System. Dr. Larkin Warner, director of the economic studies division of the foundation, said, "The region's economy can be sustained only if undeveloped water and land resources can be utilized to help replace the disappearing natural resources on which the region's cities were built."[26]

Seven eastern Oklahoma upstream lakes play a role in the navigation system. Keystone Lake, located on the Arkansas River, and six other lakes, located on tributaries, provide low-flow regulation, sediment control, flood control, domestic and industrial water supplies, recreation, and hydroelectric power. The tributary lakes are the Oologah on the Verdigris, Eufaula on the Canadian, Tenkiller Ferry on the Illinois, and Grand, Hudson, and Fort Gibson on the Grand.[27]

Hydroelectric power is generated at four dams on the project. In Oklahoma, Robert S. Kerr Lake began generating power in 1971, and Webbers Falls went on line two years later. The first tow traveled the full length of the navigation system, arriving at the Port of Catoosa on January 21, 1971.[28]

Bob sat on the platform with other dignitaries when President Richard Nixon dedicated the navigation system on June 5, 1971. The *Oklahoma Journal* noted Bob's efforts in water development, "He is carrying on the best tradition of his father…putting in endless hours of evangelization of water development in Oklahoma." The newspaper applauded OWI's slogan, "Up With Water…For People."[29]

A tow boat moves barges carrying goods down the Arkansas River. The McClellan-Kerr Arkansas River Navigation System was dedicated by President Richard Nixon in 1971.

RIGHT: Oklahoma Governor Dewey Bartlett, left, talks with Bob at the 1970 Oklahoma Water Users Association meeting at Woodward. Seven hundred people defied an ice storm to help launch the "Up With Water... for People" theme of the organization.

BELOW: Twenty eight counties in Arkansas and Oklahoma surround the Arkansas River navigation plan.

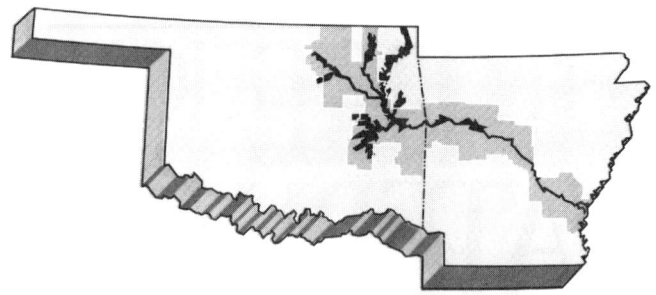

BELOW: Don McBride, left, a longtime aide to Robert S. Kerr, visits with Bob at a meeting of the Arkansas Basis Development Association. McBride later headed the Tennessee Valley Authority.

WATER CHAMPION

ABOVE: Bob, left, and Dick Godfrey, right, listen to United States Senator Jennings Randolph speak to a water forum sponsored by the Oklahoma City Chamber of Commerce.

LEFT: At the dedication of the Robert S. Kerr Lock and Dam on October 24, 1970. Left to right, Bob, Bill Kerr, Oklahoma Governor Dewey Bartlett, Oklahoma Attorney General G.T. Blankenship, United States Senator Fred Harris, Lieutenant Governor George Nigh, former First Lady Lady Bird Johnson, House Speaker Carl Albert, Kay Kerr Adair, and former President Lyndon B. Johnson.

LOU

LOU COKER WAS BORN AT HOME in the Capitol Hill section of Oklahoma City on January 24, 1937. Her parents were Lem Z. and Manolia Mae Coker.

Lou, one of ten children, was born in a small, frame house filled with rambunctious and fun-loving children at 2609 Southwest 33rd Street, a few miles from the Armour meat packing plant where her father worked until the 1950s when the plant closed.

Lou's favorite class in high school was an innovative course in economics taught by L.H. Bengston. Ahead of his time in the classroom, Bengston taught Lou and her fellow students macroeconomics and conducted hands-on experiments in the stock market. It was Lou's first introduction to the world of economics, the stock market, and business.[1]

> *I fell in love with Bob because he had the same qualities as my Dad—honesty, integrity, and abundance of love.*
>
> —LOU COKER KERR

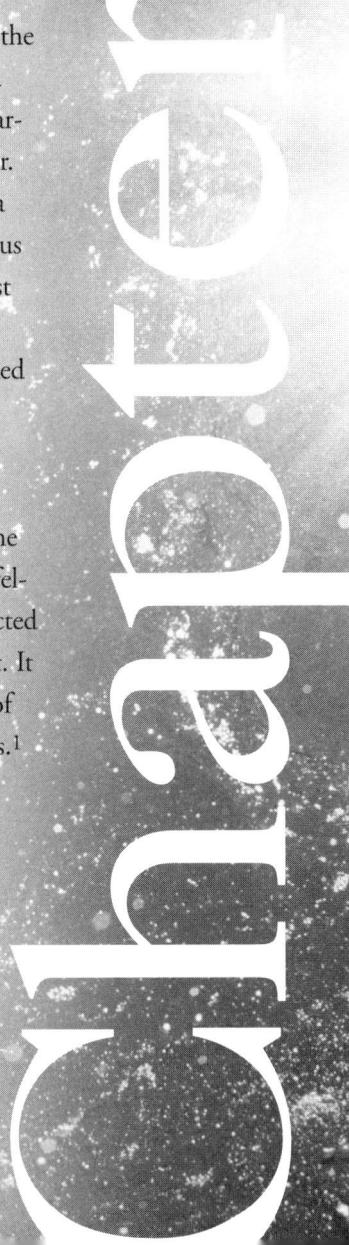

Lou's high school graduation photograph.

Because the Coker family was so large, Lou worked throughout high school to have spending money. She was a waitress, floral designer, and bookkeeper.

In 1955, Lou graduated from Capitol High School. While working at a photography shop, she became friends with a man who was a stringer for KWTV in Oklahoma City. The stringer, who sold news stories on a piece-by-piece basis to the television station, told Lou about a receptionist position open at the station. Lou applied and was hired.

In 1956, Lou met James Spears, a cameraman at KWTV. They were married in May, 1957. She continued as the receptionist for the station until her son, Steven Chris, was born on September 4, 1960, in Oklahoma City. A daughter, Laura Dyanne, was born January 5, 1967. Lou and James were divorced in 1971.

Lou had worked odd jobs outside the home as her children began school. However, in 1969, she became interested in opening a clothing store. Her friend, attorney Bill Chastain, introduced her to a banker to inquire about a loan. Lou's presentation was convincing. She talked the banker into loaning her $25,000 to open an exclusive dress shop in Shepherd Mall, a northwest Oklahoma City shopping center. Lou had always dressed impeccably, knew the latest fashion, and was extremely qualified to manage her shop she called the Jade Boutique.[2]

Running the dress shop gave Lou a great sense of the real-life business principles she had learned in theory in L.H. Bengston's class in high school. She also was aided by experience gained years before by keeping books for the flower shop. She was innovative in her buying practices and used a computer for inventory control years before other commercial establishments.[3]

When Lou first met Bob, it was love at first sight. Their friends could see the mutual love and knew they were meant for each other.

On the night before the wedding of Bob and Lou, friends gave a huge party at a hotel in Dallas, Texas. Left to right, Aubrey Kerr, Moni Boylan, Nancy Kerr, Tani Boylan, Marilynne Anderson, Breene Kerr, Shari Kerr, Jim Anderson, Joffa Kerr, Bill Kerr, Lou, Bob, and Billy Kerr.

142 MR. WATER: ROBERT S. KERR, JR.

LEFT: Bob and Lou on their wedding day in 1972.

BELOW: Bob, center, with his brothers Bill, left, and Breene, at the wedding of Bob and Lou in 1972.

ABOVE: Laura Dyanne and Steven Cris, Lou's children, were adopted by Bob. Lou said, "He loved all his children, even mine, and proved it to them by adopting them."

RIGHT: A 1973 photograph of, left to right, Valerie, Cody, Shari, Billy, and Bobby Kerr.

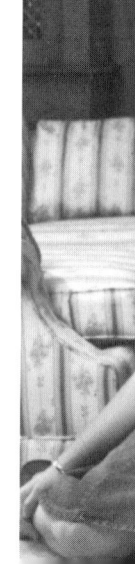

Bob was very shy and reserved. He spoke quietly and gently and won Lou's heart.

As much as Bob was quiet, Lou was funny, loud, and told great stories. During their courtship, they would spend hours on the telephone. Bob liked Lou's brothers and sisters and enjoyed visiting with them. Lou said, "They were like him, proud people who wanted nothing for themselves, but just wanted to help other people."4

Lou and Bob were married in the chapel of Highland Park United Methodist Church in Dallas on July 26, 1972. After a

brief honeymoon, Lou, Bob, Steve and Laura moved into a home on Rolling Stone Avenue in Oklahoma City.

After marrying Bob, Lou sold her dress shop and concentrated on being the best homemaker she could be. She helped Bob with his responsibilities at the Kerr Foundation that was ably managed during the 1970s by Garland Hadley, Dan Junkin, Anne Hodges Morgan, and a professional staff. Lou tagged along with Bob on trips. She said, "Being a part of his life made me feel special, complete, and happier than I had ever been in my life."5 Lou was a sponge and began gathering knowledge that would in future years allow her to manage the daily activities of the Kerr Foundation.

ABOVE: Left to right, Betty Coker, Dirk Coker, Bert Castleberry, Lou, Ann Castleberry, and Bob.

LEFT: Bob, right, presents Dr. Stanley Wagner, president of East Central State College at Ada, a check for $50,000 from the Kerr Foundation in 1971. The money was a seed grant to build a health, physical education, and activities center for the college. *Courtesy Oklahoma Publishing Company.*

THE GLOVER DEBATE

Oklahoman Carl Albert, Speaker of the United States House of Representatives, was the keynote speaker at the 1971 annual meeting of OWI in McAlester. Albert, whose influence in Congress had been vital to funding many Oklahoma water development projects, told OWI members, "With an abundant supply of clean water, man has prospered. Without it, he has died."[1]

Fresh from the success of the new Arkansas River Navigation Project, Albert said future water development in Oklahoma would require

> *If my supporting the Lukfata project casts me in the role of being irresponsible, then I am proud to be so and will continue to work in the interest of the safety and welfare of those good folks in the Glover Valley.*
>
> —Robert S. Kerr, Jr.
>
> *Dad felt an obligation to provide enduring benefit to Oklahoma.*
>
> —Shari Kerr

more than wishful thinking. Albert called for congressional support of two more navigation projects in Oklahoma. He said, "Navigation must be extended into Lake Eufaula to McAlester and up the Deep Fork to Arcadia Reservoir."[2] Albert pointed out that Oklahoma had enough water to solve all its problems, but wise planning and determination would be needed if the dream of a quality water supply for all Oklahomans was realized.[3]

Albert responded to critics who said Oklahoma needed no more reservoirs, "They simply fail to understand the full significance of water to this world…I know that what we have done thus far is good, that what we do today can be better, and that what we must do tomorrow is meet the crying need for economic prosperity…with development of higher quality water than we have known before."[4]

Most of Oklahoma's major water reservoir construction occurred after 1959. In the 1960s, Fort Cobb, Foss, Oologah, Keystone, Eufaula, Hudson, Thunderbird, Lake of the Arbuckles, Pine Creek, and Broken Bow reservoirs were completed. The 1970s brought the completion of Robert S. Kerr, Hugo, Webbers Falls, Tom Steed, Kaw, Waurika, Birch, and Optima.

Bob was happy with the completion of upstream dams across Oklahoma, but his lobbying efforts in the early 1970s centered on the proposed Lukfata Dam on Glover Creek in McCurtain County in extreme southeast Oklahoma. Undoubtedly, the Lukfata project was the most emotional and controversial fight in the history of upstream dams in Oklahoma.

Glover Creek, called "Glover River" by the hundreds of local landowners whose property was inundated by its flood waters, was the focus of water development experts and environmentalists in the 1960s and 1970s. Lukfata Lake was one of six lakes authorized by Congress in 1958 as part of a comprehensive flood control program on the upstream tributaries of Little River in southeast

Oklahoma. Lukfata, on the scenic and treacherous Glover Creek, was the only one of the six projects yet to be completed or under construction.

The destruction of the rain-swollen Glover was legendary in southeast Oklahoma. At least two or three times each year, torrents of flood waters rushed toward the Glover's convergence with Little River and on to the Red River, destroying crops and livestock and carrying away huge amounts of valuable topsoil.

Much of the opposition to Lukfata Lake came from wildlife enthusiasts who enjoyed canoeing down the last free flowing stream in the state, although a study by the Corps of Engineers found there were only 34 days during the warm months in which conditions were favorable for floating the stream.

Local landowners, such as Randy Westbrook, who lived north of the bridge across the Glover on Oklahoma Highway 3, concluded that the Glover was not a great stream to float because it was either too dry, necessitating carrying of canoes most of the day between holes of water, or dangerously full of flood water. One canoeist lost his life when trying to float the Glover after days of rain swelled the stream from its banks.

Environmentalists, after the discovery of the endangered leopard darter minnow, succeeded in delaying construction of Lukfata Lake for years. Bob wrote in the OWI newsletter, "For what seems like an eternity, we have held meetings, drafted mountains of correspondence, and cussed and discussed the problem." He said, "Lukfata Lake is needed, and it is needed now. Flood losses in the flood plains of the Glover and Little River basins on down to the Red River amount to some $2.8 million per year! That simply cannot be allowed to continue."[5]

Local residents were overwhelmingly in favor of the Lukfata Project that would be built by the Corps of Engineers. *McCurtain Gazette* publisher Jim Monroe, a former aide to United States

BELOW: Bob addresses a luncheon meeting of the Oklahoma City Chamber of Commerce. *Courtesy Oklahoma Publishing Company.*

LEFT: Bob, flanked by Congressman Carl Albert, left, and Congressman Ed Edmondson at a meeting of Oklahoma Water, Inc.

BELOW: Bob on the telephone lobbying federal legislators to support upstream dams in Oklahoma. *Courtesy Oklahoma Publishing Company.*

Senator Fred Harris, reported that 94.2 per cent of the citizens in McCurtain County responding to a survey wanted the dam built. Monroe said the pro-dam opinions in communities along the lower Glover and middle Little River Valleys, including Glover, Golden, Redland, Goodwater, and Cerrogordo, ran 100 per cent.6

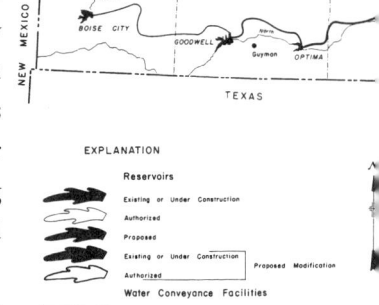

Harold Norris, chairman of the water resources committee of the Broken Bow Chamber of Commerce, said, "By covering up 1,400 acres of land in the impoundment of Glover River, we can have flood control on more than 5,800 acres of very productive land, plus enough water to irrigate 100,000 more acres." Norris concluded his remarks at an annual OWI meeting, "You have to have good water. Without water you will not have good food and fiber."7

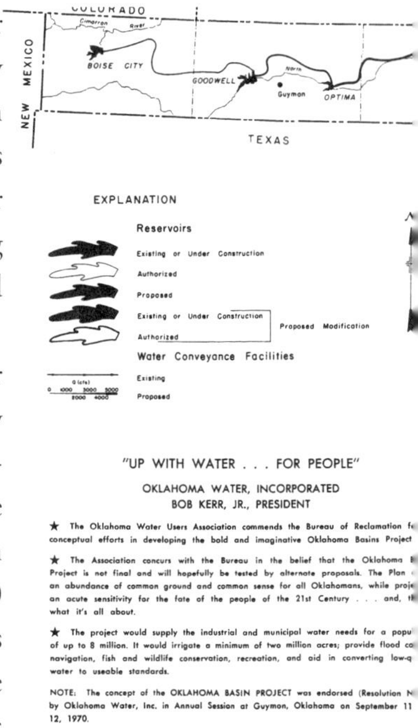

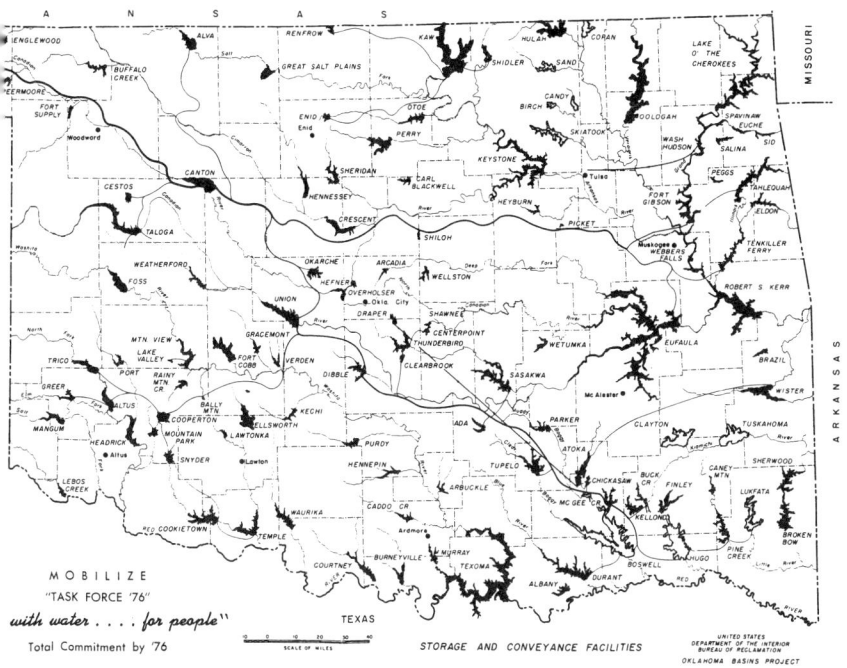

ABOVE: By 1976 many upstream dam projects had been completed in Oklahoma. This map was created by the Bureau of Reclamation depicting the Oklahoma Basins Project that would later form the core of water transfer proposals.

LEFT: Left to right, Don McBride, Bob, and Major General John Morris of the United States Corps of Engineers at a meeting of Oklahoma Water Inc.

Bob's dream of transferring surplus water from eastern Oklahoma fit perfectly with his support of reservoir construction projects such as Lukfata Lake. At a public meeting on the project, Bob said, "I'm here to tell you that the people in Oklahoma City are with you now as we always have been in your attempt to see a treacherous, though scenic stream harnessed for beneficial purposes."[8]

Bob quoted from his father's book, *Land, Wood, & Water,* about past destructive Oklahoma floods. He made a strong point that flooding along the Glover and Little rivers did not have to continue. He said, "It can and indeed must be prevented. A reservoir at the 24.5 mile site would all but eliminate this needless destruction and the threat and fear of floods that also prevent the improvement of thousands of acres of land in McCurtain County and farther east into Arkansas."[9]

Cheryl Bonner, an Idabel native and college student, spoke out in opposition to the dam, saying it would be harmful to society to change the beauty of the rugged Glover. Her song about the romantic creek and its endangered leopard darter minnow drew the attention of newspaper reporters. However, Jewel Callaham, owner of the telephone company in Broken Bow and longtime supporter of the dam on Glover, said, "You can sing about this wild river, but you don't have any idea how truly wild the river can be until you stand with a landowner who is watching his cattle herd being isolated by rising waters and there is nothing he can do to help them."[10]

Emotions ran high at public meetings on the Lukfata Lake Project. Dozens of affected landowners such as Blanche Hunter tearfully begged the Corps of Engineers to build the dam. During one seven-hour public hearing in Broken Bow, 41 persons testified concerning environmental impacts of the dam. Mrs. Frank Lewis of Tulsa told a large audience gathered in Broken Bow High School auditorium, Johnson Hall, that it would be a shame to eliminate the opportunity for her children to float the Glover.[11]

Following Mrs. Lewis was Broken Bow businessman, Bob Burke, who said, "Outsiders do not know of the wild wall of water that the river can pour out when it comes down 20 feet high and covers property and livestock."[12] Local citizens were frustrated that environmental factions, members of which lived miles away, cared little for the destruction of animals and dwellings in the local area when the river flooded. The perception was that environmentalists were meddling in local affairs and all they wanted was "a free flowing stream" they could use for recreation.

Bob recognized that any lake construction, by definition, would change the environment. "A reservoir would change things," he said, "But the moment man started building things, he has been altering the environment to suit his needs...It is man's stewardship over his natural resources that will determine the shape of the future for both his own lifestyle and his environment." Bob told one audience, "The needs of the people along the Glover Creek must be given priority. Lukfata Lake must be built!"[13]

Oklahoma United States Senators Henry Bellmon and Dewey Bartlett and United States House Speaker Carl Albert all announced their support of a dam to be built 24.5 miles above the mouth of the Glover. However, even with heavy congressional support, environmental groups who opposed the dam ultimately succeeded in convincing the Corps of Engineers to shelve the Lukfata Project on Glover Creek.

Bob, as president of WDF, surrounded himself with active, civic-minded officers. Vice presidents of the organization in 1971 were Tom Dulaney, Guy N. Keith, and Jim Pittinger. Kermit Hardwick was treasurer, V.P. Crowe was secretary, and Paul Strasbaugh was assistant secretary.

Oklahoma government leaders recognized the dedication of OWI and WDF leaders. In 1971, three OWI officers, Orville Saunders, Gerald Borelli, and Don Arch King, were appointed to the Oklahoma Water Resources Board by Governor David Hall. Two other OWI board members, Guy Keith, and Lloyd Church, were already members of the board.

Dr. Church, a Wilburton dentist, was honored by OWI and the Oklahoma legislature in 1972 as a champion of Oklahoma water development. Church was the first president of the Council of Soil Conservation Districts in Oklahoma. Bob said no one

RIGHT: "Millions Down The Drain" was the title of an Oklahoma Water, Inc. brochure that explained that each year 33 million feet of pure, fresh, high-quality water raced uncontrolled out of southeast Oklahoma to the Gulf of Mexico.

in eastern Oklahoma had more of a vision for water development than did Church.

Bert L. Castleberry was executive vice president of OWI from 1969 to 1974 and WDF manager and executive vice president of the Oklahoma Water Users Association from 1970 to 1974. When Bob could not attend a meeting of citizens interested in water development, Castleberry took his slide show on the road.

In dry western Oklahoma, local newspapers often referred to Castleberry as a "water evangelist." When he appeared at a public meeting at the high school auditorium in Mangum, Castleberry responded to critics who called Bob and Oklahoma Water, Inc.

MILLIONS DOWN THE DRAIN

"those crazy people with a four billion dollar dream, trying to run water uphill." Castleberry said, "Bob Kerr's father thought that barges could be brought up the rivers to Catoosa, and it has been accomplished. Franklin D. Roosevelt thought that we could eliminate polio if everyone gave a dime, and 25 years later it was a wonderful reality. They dreamed of water canals in California and now they are carrying water."[14]

Appearances by Bob and Castleberry received much advance publicity in water-hungry parts of the state. Before a public meeting, billed as an "educational meeting for general information on the Water Users Association," the newspaper in Granite urged people to go to the meeting, noting, "Plan to attend because water is everyone's business."[15]

Recognizing Castleberry's water resource knowledge and integrity, Governor David Hall

LEFT: In addition to dozens of speeches by Bob and other Oklahoma Water, Inc. officials each year, the organization produced brochures and information packets about Oklahoma water issues.

appointed him to the Oklahoma Water Resources Board in 1974. Casteleberry died in 1977 after a year-long battle with cancer.

In August, 1971, Colonel Vernon W. Pinkey, who had been the Corps of Engineers' top man in the Tulsa District for three years, became executive vice president of the Arkansas Basin Development Association (ABDA), an important group that presented a strong front for the states along the Arkansas River. John D. Mayo, Glade R. Kirkpatrick, Charles B. Gannaway, Jr., George H. Gates, Marcus R. Tower, W.E. Bender, Jacques Cunningham, and L.W. Grant, Jr. were members of the 1971 ABDA board.

Bob realized the importance of the ABDA and intervened when Pinkey was concerned that Governor Hall might replace all veteran Oklahoma representatives on the Arkansas River Basin Interstate Committee with new people who had little knowledge of Oklahoma's water needs. After discussions with Hall, Bob reported to Pinkey that even though Hall wanted to put some of his people on the interstate committee, he promised he would select men who shared OWI's views on water development.[16]

In 1972, Bob became heavily involved in fighting new federal regulations that proposed to change the way Congress and the Corps of Engineers evaluated the economic feasibility of water resource projects. The new regulations, announced by the federal Water Resources Council, were in the words of Congressman Ed Edmondson, "an administrative attempt to circumvent clear decisions of both Congress and President Richard Nixon."[17]

For two decades, the government had used a discount rate of 5 3/8 percent to calculate the future economic feasibility of water resources development. In essence, the discount rate was the interest rate that the federal government could earn on its funds if not used for water development projects. The Water Resources Council recommended the rate be hiked to seven percent. Bob said, "Any increase in the discount rate will emasculate Oklahoma's magnificent water development plans and will destroy our ability to affix an umbilical cord to the world market."[18] Unwritten was Bob's fear that projects such as the Central Oklahoma Project and water projects at Candy, Clayton, Boswell, Shidler, Skiatook, and Tuskahoma would be found not economically feasible using the new discount rate.

Bob was able to mount a strong political campaign against the Water Resources Council's actions. He enlisted support from Oklahoma's United States Senators Henry Bellmon and Fred Harris, Illinois Senator Adlai Stevenson III, and Colorado Senator Peter Dominick, who wrote, "I question the wisdom of retarding water resources development at a time when our rapidly increasing population is placing corresponding demands on the nation's limited water supplies."[19]

Bob was one of five individual plaintiffs and a dozen regional and national water development organizations that filed suit in federal court in the District of Columbia to block the National Water Resources Council's actions.

The political and legal pressure worked. President Richard Nixon asked the Water Resources Council to delay any drastic change in the discount rate until congressional committees could complete a full investigation on how America would calculate the benefit of future water development projects. The discount rate was ultimately raised, but in steps, and to less than the seven percent recommended.

Bob's efforts in water development were recognized outside Oklahoma again in 1974 when he was elected to the board of directors of the National Waterways Conference (NWC) during the organization's annual meeting in Memphis, Tennessee. The NWC was committed to providing citizens of the United States with a greater understanding of the widespread benefits of the American waterways system.

There was a changing of the guard in the offices of OWI in 1974. Ronn W. Cupp, the assistant to Bert Castleberry, became executive vice president of OWI and manager of the Water Development Foundation of Oklahoma, Incorporated. Cupp, a native of Altus, Oklahoma, had graduated from Oklahoma State University (OSU) before serving three years in the United States Air Force.

At the tender age of 25, Cupp was introduced to the famous Kerr pause. In his second interview with Bob, Cupp was anxious and did not know how to deal with the pause. However, Bob was gracious and erased any intimidation that Cupp felt sitting across the table from a member of the Kerr family of which he had great respect. The interview went well, and Cupp was hired.

Bob hired Cupp because he was impressed with Cupp's military background. Bob had never forgotten his own training at the New Mexico Military Institute and wanted his right hand man to have the acumen of a good military officer. Because Cupp was an OSU graduate, he also became the group's "token Aggie."

Quickly after taking over the every day operations of OWI and WDF, Cupp became a director of the Arkansas Basin Development Association and vice chairman of the Water Development Council of the Oklahoma City Chamber of Commerce.

Cupp was thrown into the midst of major water projects. He realized he had gotten himself into a hornet's nest regarding Lukfata Lake, and went to the work with Paul Strasbaugh, Guy Keith, and Dr. Larkin Warner to counter Corps of Engineers' negative reports on the Central Oklahoma Project.

From Cupp's first day on the job, Bob became his mentor. Both often quoted Will Rogers and Cupp learned of Bob's fondness for Winston Churchill. Cupp used his journalism degree to draft speeches for Bob as the topic of water development in Oklahoma rose to near the top of political discussions in the state.

On one of his first trips with Bob, Cupp learned how Bob had totally committed to memory the vast amount information about water development. They met Muskogee banker John Hannah and changed cars for the short ride to a speech at Fort Gibson. Bob left his copy of the speech in his car in Muskogee, and asked Cupp for another copy. Cupp did not have an extra copy, and Bob gave his entire speech from memory. Cupp remembered, "It was a flawless presentation, and I always carried extra copies of his speeches after that day."

Chapter 10

DEVELOPING A WATER PLAN

BOB TRIED TO CONVEY TO AUDIENCES across the state the urgency of finding ways to move surplus water. He said, "The opportunity to build such a project will not always be an exercisable option. It will predictably disappear with the passing of time."[1]

As early as 1971, Bob began talking publicly about transferring eastern Oklahoma water to central and western portions of the state. He pointed to a 1965 study by the Bureau of Reclamation, the "Oklahoma

> *About the best way to claim water that comes from your state is to grab it off before it gets out of your state.*
>
> —WILL ROGERS
>
> *Never in its history has Oklahoma cried out so loudly for bold, imaginative, and selfless leadership in water development.*
>
> —ROBERT S. KERR, JR.

Basins Project," that could be used as the framework for a statewide water inventory and conveyance system that could move as much as 11 million acre feet of water annually.

The specific plan was to build a transport system of 1,990 miles of concrete aqueducts, pipelines, and siphons, 89 pump stations or lifts, and 69 new reservoirs. There needed to be two major aqueduct systems—one from northeast to northwest Oklahoma and a canal from southeast to southwest Oklahoma. Bob estimated such a grandiose water transfer plan would cost more than four billion dollars. He cited economic estimates that adequate water for irrigation in water-starved sections of the state could triple Oklahoma's $1-billion-a-year agricultural industry. He quoted an Oklahoma State University agricultural economic study that concluded that for every dollar spent on the farm, a three to four dollar increase can be expected in the general economy. In other words, Bob was convinced that water transfer could grow the Oklahoma economy by more than $10 billion a year.

Irrigation was only one segment of the benefits of a water transfer plan. Other benefits were sufficient industrial and municipal water supplies, recreational development, navigation, and flood control.

Oklahoma Governor Hall echoed Bob's support for a massive water transfer plan, calling it, "an excellent plan that would result in opening a frontier in the western sections of Oklahoma."[2]

OWI called for the legislature to create a state water authority or commission that would have authority to finance, build, and operate all facilities necessary to transfer water. Bob said time was a major stumbling block to the development of Oklahoma water for Oklahomans. In speeches across the state, he said:

> Recent federal policies indicate a shift toward regional development of water resources. Oklahoma is the prime

water hole for the Southwest. If she doesn't develop her own water, the federal government will step in sooner or later and do it for her. The High Plains of Texas and New Mexico and sections of nearby states thirst for water. It seems only logical that Oklahoma should develop her own water resources, and reap the benefits of any transfer to other states.³

Armed with information from Bob and OWI, many of the state's newspapers began calling for legislative solutions to studying the water transfer idea. Bob Lee Kidd, Jr., publisher of *The LeFlore County Sun* in Poteau, recognized the controversial nature of water transfer:

> We have profit-sharing, revenue-sharing, and many other forms of sharing but all too many people in eastern Oklahoma get wild-eyed and almost verbally insulting when the idea of water-sharing is brought up. And I think this attitude is brought about because a lack of information between the pros and cons, a misrepresented idea of a very feasible and great idea...
>
> There are those in eastern Oklahoma who scream, "They can't have our water! Why should western Oklahoma have our water?" A member of the state legislature from eastern Oklahoma counties north of us ranted and snorted in a Sallisaw meeting recently about "they're not gonna' get any of my water. They think Bob Kerr, Jr. is a meddling nut.⁴

Kidd, a longtime newspaperman in the heart of water-rich LeFlore County, recognized the good things about Bob's water transfer ideas, "The plan, in a nutshell, is to capture what water we lose, over and above that which we can store, to the Mississippi River, and pump it back to central and western

Oklahoma reservoirs from where it will be redistributed when needed. There is absolutely no rhyme nor reason for people in eastern Oklahoma to rise up in hypocritical self-righteousness and yell, 'Let 'em get their own water!'"5

The value of water, as a tool for economic development, was considered to be a major argument in convincing the legislature to tackle the controversial business of studying water transfer. John Steiger, retired manager of civic affairs for Cities Service Company, and vice chairman of the Caucus on Eastern Oklahoma's Future, wrote in the *Tulsa Tribune*, "Eastern and western Oklahoma should join forces to keep Oklahoma's water for Oklahomans…Oklahoma is growing. It will be bringing in new water-using industries. It has great potential for developing Garden-of-Eden truck farms based on irrigation…the only apparent way is to come up with a people-involving, municipality-involving, regional-involving, and state-involving statistical study of present water usage—and project those needs over the next decade…Then, extrapolate these first-decade figures into an estimate of our water needs over the next 50 years…Without such a statistical base, our government is at a loss to defend Oklahoma's water rights should the dividing of the waters become a federal issue."6

One of Bob's closest allies in the fight to force to the state to develop a comprehensive water transfer plan was Dr. Bernice Crockett of Durant, chairman of the Oklahoma Water Council on Education. Crockett, as OWI's education director, kept busy

Bob talks about development of Oklahoma water resources at a 1973 meeting of the Oklahoma Press Association.

by traveling to every corner of the state to hold educational institutes. Crockett also headed up OWI's essay contest program in which high school students entered a statewide competition in writing essays on the value of water. Crocket strongly believed the only way Oklahomans would ultimately be sold on a water transfer plan was for teenagers, future voters, to become acquainted with water development.

OWI launched a vigorous campaign in the state press to raise awareness of the need for a water plan. Press releases, with facts and opinions under the banner of "Calvin Says," were sent to all newspapers and radio and television stations in the state. The campaign was a success—many daily and weekly newspapers used the "Calvin Says" logo and quotes.

A number of state legislators also expressed interest in getting behind Bob's efforts. Attending the 1971 OWI annual meeting were House Speaker Rex Privett, Maramec; Representatives Howard Cotner, Altus; Barbour Cox, Chandler; Marvin McKee, Guymon; Hugh Sandlin, Holdenville; Wayne Sanguin, Hugo; David Stratton, Clinton; and Ray Trent, Del City. State senators present were Bryce Baggett, Oklahoma City; Gilmer Capps, Snyder; Herschal Crow, Altus; John Dahl, Bartlesville; Don Ferrell, Chandler; Leon Field, Texhoma; Clem McSpadden, Claremore; George Miller, Ada; Robert Murphy, Stillwater; and Gene Stipe, McAlester. The legislators took part in a panel discussion on ways and means to finance a statewide comprehensive water plan.7

Dr. Lloyd Church of Wilburton, left, was a staunch supporter of Bob and his efforts to develop Oklahoma water resources. In this photograph, Dr. Church and Governor Dewey Bartlett wait to speak to a meeting of Oklahoma Water, Inc.

A 1973 study by the Bureau for Business and Economic Research at the University of Oklahoma supported Bob's assertions that water would be short in central and western Oklahoma in the following half-century. The study predicted that water shortages, without federal approval of new reservoirs, would curtail the economic potential of Oklahoma by $1.2 billion by 1990, $2.3 billion by 2000, and $17.8 billion by 2070. The OU study came on the heels of a Corps of Engineers report that estimated additional water for irrigation in southwest Oklahoma could increase the state's economy by $5 billion over a 50-year period.[8]

In August, 1973, the Kerr Foundation expressed an interest in funding a fulltime program of support for research on various issues affecting the Oklahoma economy. They hired Larkin Warner, an economist at OU, to become director of the Kerr Foundation's Economic Studies Division, a post he held for the next five years. Warner remembered, "Bob was totally committed to using his influence and the Foundation's resources for the good of the state."[9]

By 1973, pushing for a comprehensive water plan was such a hot topic that OWI meetings became well-attended. Water transfer was a dirty word for some eastern Oklahoma politicians and state officials who wanted to stay out of the crossfire between eastern Oklahoma residents who had the water and those in western Oklahoma who needed the water. At the October, 1973 annual OWI meeting at the Black Angus Motel in Poteau, Forrest Nelson, director of the Oklahoma Water Resources Board, said there was no urgency to develop a comprehensive water plan.[10]

That view was strongly debated and there was a sense that the state's water groups were divided on a single approach. Bert Castleberry said, "Let's put it all out on the table and call a spade, a spade…Be it east, west, north, or south, the people are not opposed to optimal water development. The buck stops in this room. Our house is out of order. We are not in step with each other. We must first close the ranks within the water groups."[11]

Castleberry was upset that the Arkansas Development Basin Association had failed to publicly support OWI's call for the state legislature to pass Senate Bill 200 that would create a statewide conveyance commission. Bob said of the bill that was filed in February, 1973, "It is an enormously bold, modern, and forward looking piece of water legislation…it is the first step toward preventing a federal grab of Oklahoma's water."[12] Senator Herschal Crow of Altus and Representative Spencer Bernard of Rush Springs were principal legislative authors of the bill.

Reporting to OWI members about the subsequent legislative death of Senate Bill 200, Bob wrote, "The visionary bill was alternately praised, damned, libeled, slandered, and finally emasculated. To say it was misunderstood is an understatement."[13]

Even though the Oklahoma Water Resources Board had been authorized by the legislature in 1963 to develop a long-range water plan for the state, nothing had materialized by 1974. During the legislative session that year, Senate Bill 510, a watered-down version of the previous year's Senate Bill 200, was passed and signed into law by Governor Hall.

The bill directed the OWRB to prepare the first phase of the Oklahoma Comprehensive Water Plan (Water Plan). The legislation authorized a working study of the economics and engineering of water resource development in the southern 33 counties of Oklahoma. For the remaining 44 counties, the OWRB was to use existing research and data to determine if additional study was required.[14]

Bob was happy that the legislature did something, but he believed Senate Bill 510 was anemic. Senate Bill 200 had clearly stated that only excess and surplus water would ever be removed from an area of the state for redistribution to other locations. Citizens in the area of origin had absolute authority over "beneficial use" of its water. The bill also called for the creation of a Water Transportation Commission, appointed by the governor, to oversee water transfer. The broad, sweeping powers given to the Water Transportation Commission raised concerns among many legislators, and authorization for such an entity to control water transfer was not included in Senate Bill 510 that passed the legislature in 1974.[15]

The OWRB was under the firm control of executive director Forrest Nelson, a longtime public servant. Nelson was appointed to Governor Raymond Gary's water study committee in 1955. When the legislature created the OWRB, he was named assistant director. When executive director Frank Raab retired in 1967, Nelson took over the reins of the agency.

Nelson deftly guided his professional staff toward development of a water plan. State agencies, universities, and many federal agencies were called upon to provide input and funding for creation of the plan. Substate planning districts, the Kiamichi Economic Development District (KEDDO), the Southern Oklahoma Development Association (SODA), and the Economic Resources Development Association (ERDA), in cooperation with the Corps of Engineers, provided population projections and helped target future water requirements. Open meetings were held throughout the state to obtain citizens' comments.

The hot topic of water development was passed from outgoing Governor Hall to newly-elected Governor David L. Boren in 1975. In April, 1975, a draft copy of "Phase I—Oklahoma Comprehensive Water Plan" was distributed to members of the OWRB. Because a majority of the members of the board were Bob's close friends and members of OWI, Bob was allowed to review the draft.

The Phase I plan for Oklahoma's southern 33 counties was intended to provide a 50-year guide for an orderly and coordinated approach to developing the region's water resources. The Phase I plan recognized that most water requirements in the southern counties would be met by ground water sources and the 31 major reservoirs and lakes in the area.[16]

Phase I contained sweeping recommendations regarding water transfer. The "Interconnected System" provided for transferring surplus water to central and southwest Oklahoma. Specifically, 487,000 acre-feet of water would be delivered by pipelines, aqueducts, and pumping plants to central Oklahoma, primarily Oklahoma City, for municipal and industrial use. More than 700,000 acre-feet would be transferred to southwestern Oklahoma, mostly for irrigation of arid farmland.[17]

Initial construction costs for the Interconnected System was pegged at $1.4 billion. Economists estimated that water delivered to central Oklahoma would cost about 19 cents for 1,000 gallons while water delivered to terminal reservoirs in the southwest part of the state would cost 33 cents per 1,000 gallons.[18]

The Oklahoma Water Resources Board agreed that the initial cost of construction and the estimated $124 million annual cost to operate the Interconnected System were justified from both economic and engineering standpoints. Most of the reservoirs needed to carry out the plan were either built or under construction. Water from Hugo, Clayton, Boswell, and Tuskahoma reservoirs would be transferred to West Elm Creek and Stanley Draper in central Oklahoma and Verden, Altus, Tom Steed, Snyder, Mangum, Foss, and Fort Cobb reservoirs in southwestern Oklahoma. Hugo, Draper, Altus, Tom Steed, Foss, and Fort Cobb were in place. Clayton and Boswell were under construction, Tuskahoma was authorized, and West Elm, Mangum, Snyder, and Verden were proposed.[19]

Total length of the water conveyance system would be 389 miles. Water would be lifted 1,653 feet from the eastern side of the state to its destination in southwest Oklahoma.[20]

"Without a viable water distribution plan for the future," the report said, "the economy of the entire state, with its agriculture, agri-business, and related industries, could suffer." The Phase I report concluded, "The state must exercise strong leadership in guiding the role of water resource development in Oklahoma. The federal agencies should be encouraged to construct portions of the Plan which can be justified from a federal standpoint but the state must never become dependent upon the federal government for implementation of the Plan."[21]

The Phase I plan also called for a quick completion of Phase II, a study of water needs and surplus water transfer possibilities for the remaining counties in Oklahoma.

Phase I received a cold shoulder from many legislators and political leaders who were frightened by the multi-billion dollar price tag of moving water from eastern to western Oklahoma. The state legislature failed to authorize any of the plan's recommendations except to authorize the OWRB to prepare a similar plan for the remaining 44 counties in Oklahoma. Michael R. Melton, who was charged with developing the comprehensive water plan, suggested to the press that the impact study would take two years and would cost $250,000.[22] Melton was overly optimistic on both counts.

WATER FOR ECONOMIC DEVELOPMENT

IN 1975, Bob was invited to address President Richard Nixon's Regional Forum on Domestic Policy in Austin, Texas. Assisted by OWI executive vice president Ronn Cupp, Bob developed a position paper to be submitted to the federal forum.

> *Without the development of our natural resources, energy, mineral and water, there can be no economic growth, no viable social policy, and certainly no community development in America.*
>
> —ROBERT S. KERR, JR.
>
> *Never was I in a meeting with Bob that his presence, just by being there, did not add purpose to what we were doing. When he spoke, everyone listened, even with a soft and almost humble delivery.*
>
> —DEAN SCHIRF

Bob said resource development should be the central concern of a national domestic policy. He pointed to the recent Arab oil embargo that spotlighted America's growing dependence on foreign oil and lack of a national policy on energy.

Specifically, Bob said, "Water resources development is the key to a viable natural resource policy." He told the Texas audience, "If any one thing has limited the development of mid-America to date, it has been a lack of water development." He cited studies that talked about the uneven distribution of water and the lack of federal incentives to urge states to do something about it.[1]

Bob accused the federal government of wielding "too heavy a hand" in water resource development. Instead, he urged the federal government to allow states to develop their own water resources. He said he was growing tired of the federal bureaucracy, "There was a time when if a local problem arose, a little American ingenuity would be applied, and sooner or later, the problem would be solved. That time seems to have long since passed. Today, when a problem arises, we rush to send a delegation to Washington because that's the place where all the important decisions are made."[2]

Bob used the forum in Texas to slam the federal Water Resources Council for continuing to promulgate new and more stringent rules for evaluating the economic feasibility of water projects. He said, "I believe the Water Resources Council has done irreparable damage to water resources development in the country…thanks to the many restraints placed upon water resources programs, water resources development has become the step-child of the nation's resource development program."[3]

Bob urged a huge federal investment in water development. "It would begin paying dividends almost immediately," he said, "It would pay large returns through creation of jobs, stabilization of the economy, and encouragement of fiscal responsibility, and would act as a magnet for private investment." He concluded that federal funding of state-controlled water resource projects would "prime the pump" for large scale economic development.[4]

In 1976, Bob was appointed by the OWRB to chair the Oklahoma Weather Modification Advisory Committee. A new federal law mandated that the United States Secretary of Commerce study weather modification technology and its implications and develop a national weather modification policy. Serving with Bob on the committee were Dick Hamilton of Harmon, Representative Bob Parris of Sallisaw, Wayman Cornelsen of Fairview, Ferdie Deering of Oklahoma City, Senator Bob Funston of Broken Arrow, Paul Hitch of Guymon, C.R. Holden of Tulsa, Nelson Doughty of Altus, and Jess Stratton of Clinton.[5]

Bob was also appointed as a member of the Oklahoma delegation of the Arkansas Basin Interstate Committee, joining Fred Turner of McAlester, Senator Funston, Glade Kirkpatrick of Tulsa, and George Downs, Jr. of Bartlesville.

OWI continued to be the driving force behind the development of a comprehensive water plan for Oklahoma. Bob, Ronn Cupp, and Dr. Bernice Crockett appeared at dozens of civic clubs, meetings, conferences, and workshops. In 1976, OWI prepared 325 news releases, 1,250 special news releases under the "Calvin Says" headline, three newsletters, and granted numerous radio and television interviews.

Bob considered 1977 and 1978 to be perhaps the most eventful years of the decade, at least, waterwise. Water development conferences were held throughout the state, clamoring for public support for the statewide water plan that was still in the drafting stages at the OWRB.

After a meeting in Henryetta, at which western Oklahoma water leaders were welcomed for discussions with eastern Oklahomans, Bob was encouraged that a turning point had been reached. In a press release following the Water Resources Conference, sponsored by the Caucus on Eastern Oklahoma's Future, he said, "The significance of the conference is that some 150 persons met in eastern Oklahoma to discuss a subject which many times in the past would have made the blood of any true blue eastern Oklahoman boil. I believe the general consensus was that eastern Oklahomans are quite willing to share the bountiful water surplus with which they are blessed if they are guaranteed first rights and area of origin protection, and if they are given a strong voice in the how's, why's, and wherefore's."[6]

One reason for Bob's optimism was his admiration for and excellent working relationship with Governor Boren, who in January, 1978, proposed to the legislature a plan, Senate Bill 625, that would create the Oklahoma Water Development Authority. Such an authority, long Bob's dream, would build and manage any future water transfer system in the state. Even though the bill narrowly was defeated in the legislature, Bob called it, "notice that water development has re-emerged as a predominant issue in Oklahoma."[7]

Senate Bill 625 provided a mechanism that would have allowed communities and local agencies to obtain grants and low-interest loans for water development projects. Bob said of the governor's effort, "Boren became the first Oklahoma governor since Robert S. Kerr to sponsor truly significant water development legislation." OWI executive vice president Ronn Cupp said, "Senate Bill 625 was devoured by that old green-eyed political dragon which thrives on conflict between eastern and western Oklahoma, a dragon which must be slain forever if Oklahoma is to develop her water resources to the fullest."[8]

Failure of the legislature to move forward on a comprehensive state water plan drew the ire of the press in 1977. An editorial in *The Daily Oklahoman* said, "What Oklahoma didn't need was the disclosure this week that completion of the comprehensive water plan may be delayed for two years…That initial part of the plan has gathered dust in the legislature for nearly two years, stymied mostly by opposition from eastern and southeastern regional interests who fear that the proposed water transfer might jeopardize their future growth."[9]

The *Oklahoman* editorial continued, "Further delays imperil Oklahoma's future economic growth and progress. Every year brings a further withdrawal of diminishing groundwater supplies in many of the more arid western and southwestern counties…Failure to adopt any plan could preclude Oklahoma from having any say about how and when and where its surplus water will be used."[10]

In a feature article titled "Water, Water Everywhere And Not A Drop To Share?" *Oklahoma Monthly* magazine criticized state leaders for not reaching agreement on water sharing. "The concern felt by panhandle ranchers and farmers," the magazine article said, "is that if they do not devise a method to make use of the state's surplus water, other surrounding states may seize the opportunity."11

Bob feared that farmers and ranchers in dry west Texas might covet Oklahoma water someday. The United States Department of Agriculture estimated that 40 percent of Texas' cotton production was on irrigated land, drawing its water from the Ogallala aquifer, the groundwater formation than spanned the Great Plains from Nebraska southward into the Oklahoma and Texas panhandles.

In 1976, Governor Boren and the governors of five other High Plains states formed the High Plains Study Council, a conduit for $6 million in federal dollars to study what the future held for the Ogallala formation which provided water for more than 20 percent of the nation's irrigated lands. In addressing a group of interested water users from the Oklahoma Panhandle, Bob said, "The warnings about the possible expropriation of Oklahoma water are not fabrications, nor are they scare tactics or attempts to stir up emotional sentiment among the citizenry."12

Governor Boren tried to apply pressure on the legislature to complete the comprehensive statewide water plan. In a letter to House Speaker William P. Willis and Senate President Pro Tempore Gene Howard, Boren wrote, "I respectfully request that the Legislative Council study the total needs of water development...Without exaggerating, we may see a day in which a barrel of water will be as precious as a barrel of oil...Even in eastern Oklahoma which is considered relatively rich in water, it is estimated that one-third of all rural residents lack safe, dependable community water supplies. Yet Oklahoma continues to allow vast quantities of our water to flow into other states."13

A great deal of the controversy surrounding a statewide water plan had to do with irrigation, because most of the water exported from eastern Oklahoma would go for that purpose. A 1977 irrigation survey conducted by Oklahoma State University found that less than 900,000 acres were irrigated the previous year of the more than 5 million acres the Bureau of Reclamation said were suitable for irrigation in the state. "Even if half that land can be irrigated with surplus water," Bob told an audience in Altus, "it will be the greatest lift to the Oklahoma economy ever."14

Much of Bob's time in 1977 and 1978 was spent on support for the construction of two new reservoirs in Oklahoma—Arcadia Lake east of Edmond and McGee Creek Reservoir on Muddy Boggy Creek in Atoka County. Both were critical to supply future water needs for central Oklahoma.

For years, congressional approval had been sought for both reservoirs. McGee Creek had been authorized by Congress in 1976. Slowly, but surely, with the support of Oklahoma's congressional delegation, the projects moved closer to funding. However, in 1977, the future of the McGee Creek project was threatened by differences among Oklahoma's delegation.

Congressman Wes Watkins was angered by Senator Henry Bellmon's failure to include any future funding in the Senate appropriations bill for the shelved Lukfata project on Glover Creek. Bellmon had reversed his stand on the Lukfata project, citing a poor economic feasibility study and continuing opposition by environmentalists.

When Bob complained about Bellmon's opposition to Lukfata, Bellmon wrote to him, "It is not my intention to attempt to favor foreclosing construction on Lukfata.

Rather I feel that the federal resources now available should be applied to projects which have a higher benefit cost ratio and for which there is a greater need. Delaying Lukfata until water is needed for Oklahoma's development would seem to be a wise course of action."[15] In retrospect, the Lukfata project was already dead and would never be revived.

However, Watkins privately told supporters that he wanted the Lukfata Dam built and that he was ready to pull his support for the McGee Creek reservoir that would provide much-needed water for Oklahoma City and central Oklahoma. The five-county Oklahoma City metropolitan area was expected to include more than one million people by 1985 and would need the water provided by McGee Creek. There was no time for delay.

Fortunately, Orlie Boehler, executive director of SODA, the substate planning district in southern Oklahoma, and LeRoy Jackson, administrative assistant to Congressman Watkins, maneuvered a series of meetings to solidify Watkins' support for both McGee Creek, in his district, and Lake Arcadia.[16]

At a public meeting at Central State University in Edmond, Bob spoke on behalf of the Water Development Foundation of Oklahoma. Recognizing that Arcadia Lake had been an environmental and political yo-yo since its authorization in 1970, Bob said, "The needs and justification for the lake are obvious. Edmond, one of Oklahoma's fastest-growing suburban communities, needs the water. Oklahomans living along the Deep Fork need the flood protection, and central Oklahoma, an area that will contain more than a million people by the year 2000, needs the recreational opportunities Arcadia Lake would provide."[17]

Bob addressed his comments to opponents of the lake, some of whom were losing their land. He said, "It is a peculiar trademark of democracies such as ours that individuals are sometimes asked to make personal sacrifices for the public good. In many cases, this involves giving up a farm or perhaps a home, to allow for the creation of a public facility such as a park, highway, or a waterworks project, from which we all may derive benefit from time to time."[18]

After public hearings and more bureaucratic wrangling, both Arcadia Lake and McGee Creek were funded and constructed, assuring central Oklahoma of an adequate water supply for decades to come.

OWI fostered active participation in water projects by the state's lake associations, made up of groups of local leaders who were interested in the development and protection of their reservoirs. From the local lake associations came some of OWI's most vocal supporters such as David Norris of the Broken Bow Lake Association, Don Shotwell of the Lake Eufaula Association, William Brooks of the Fort Gibson Lake Association, James Larson of the Grand Lake Association, David Beard of the Kaw Lake Association, L.W. Anderson of the Lake Texoma Association, and Bob Stewart of the Lake Tenkiller Association.

Bob became quite concerned about the Carter administration's water development policies in 1977, especially the Water Resources Council and its continuing hike in the discount rate that affected the feasibility of water projects. Where President Nixon had helped stave off huge raises in the discount rate, Carter did not. Bob wrote the president, "I am skeptical of and somewhat alarmed at your attempts to create a shambles of a program which has proven itself again and again, all in the name of reform, and under the guises of economic and environmental issues." Bob told the president that Oklahoma had been a prime beneficiary of a progressive water policy and that planned changes would be devastating to future water projects.[19]

Even though a comprehensive state water plan was still at least three years away from release, education efforts of Dr. Bernice Crockett and OWI about the benefits of water transfer paid dividends. An example was a 1977 editorial in the *Coalgate Record/Register* by publisher George B. Hill:

> We are in an emergency situation in Oklahoma but most citizens don't realize it. The Ogallala formation, which supplies most of the irrigation water to the dry panhandle and most of western Oklahoma, is going to run dry in 20 years…So time's a wasting…Cities and towns with surpluses could transfer water to cities and towns in need of water. Irrigation districts could be established to make utmost use of farming potential. The possibilities of floods, which we have every spring, could be reduced...
>
> It is too bad that most citizens will only be able to see the advantages of a water transfer system and storage system when we have our next big drought—and we will have one. We always have. Even more important, if the Ogallala runs dry before we establish a water transfer system in Oklahoma, the desert that is created in western and northwestern Oklahoma will make the dusty bowl days of the 1930s look like a child's sand pile.[20]

The message about the importance of water development in Oklahoma was getting through, even in water-rich eastern Oklahoma towns like Coalgate.

In 1979, a new Oklahoma governor, George Nigh, wholeheartedly endorsed Oklahoma Water Inc.'s drive for a statewide water plan. In his inaugural address, Nigh said:

> The need for a comprehensive water plan is critical…We have no greater obligation to the posterity of our state. We must assure that the needs of those who presently capture water are protected. We must protect not only the present needs, but future needs that can be defined…It is our challenge today, not tomorrow, to cast aside parochialism and fashion a water plan we can grow with. If we protect the water of those who have it, and share the excess with those who need it, Oklahoma has more than enough for us all to enjoy today and for as many tomorrows as we can envision.[21]

Also in 1979, President Carter released his long-awaited national water policy. Bob did not question the need for the federal government to make a definitive statement on water policy, but he strongly disagreed with the emphasis on conservation. A central theme of the policy was summarized in the statement, "Using water more efficiently is often cheaper and less damaging to the environment than developing additional supplies. While increases in supply will still be necessary, these reforms place emphasis on water conservation and make clear that this now is a national priority."[22]

Bob saw the handwriting on the wall. The great successes Oklahoma had enjoyed in winning hundreds of millions of dollars for water reservoir projects in the past would be more difficult in the future. He knew it would be harder to obtain federal funding for either planning or constructing water projects.

Of the new federal emphasis on water conservation, rather than constructing new reservoirs, Bob believed the national water policy to be bad for southwestern and western states. He said, "Conservation is important…However, the nation can no more conserve its way to water prosperity than it can to oil prosperity. Conservation and development must go hand-in-hand, and the emphasis on each should be equal."[23]

Bob could never pinpoint any specific reason for President Carter's attitude toward water development. He liked Carter and chalked the bad water policy up to "poor advice," or perhaps Carter, being from Georgia, "did not really understand the relation of water to the social and economic affairs of the western and southwestern states."[24]

Bob did not spend his time talking about water exclusively in Oklahoma. In 1979, he addressed the closing luncheon session of the National Waterways Conference in Nashville, Tennessee. He talked of new federal reforms and tough going that lay ahead, "Water resources development has never been easy. But unless there is a shift in national policy, water projects will soon become an extinct species. They are already endangered."[25]

Bob challenged the elite of the nation's water development leaders:

> The wise management of our water resources is too important to America's well being to let bureaucratic obstacles get in the way. No longer can we tolerate stop-and-go, stop-and-study, stop-and-sue policies which stifle water resources development. If

America does not wake up to this fact, I fear we will soon have not only an energy crisis—but a water crisis as well. And, as far as I know, water is one thing we cannot buy from the Arabs.[26]

Chapter 12
QUEST FOR THE SENATE

Even though Bob had backed away from previous campaigns for the United States Senate and governor of Oklahoma, he was interested in politics and often played a behind-the-scenes role in campaigns. In 1978, he was active in the election of his oldest son, RSK III, to a seat in the Oklahoma House of Representatives. The younger Kerr, a Democrat, was elected to the District 86 seat in Oklahoma County vacated by Kerr's friend, David Hood. RSK III, who had worked alongside his father for a decade at OWI, announced that a comprehensive water plan should be at the top of the state's priority.

> *Running against someone named Kerr in Oklahoma was tough. I found myself campaigning down Kerr Avenue or speaking in Kerr Pavilion or Kerr Arena in towns across the state.*
> —Andrew M. "Andy" Coats

OWI executive director Ronn Cupp, left, and Robert S. Kerr III look over data being developed by OWI for inclusion in an eventual comprehensive water plan for Oklahoma.

Also in 1978, Bob endorsed State Senator Bob Funston of Broken Arrow in the Democratic primary for governor of Oklahoma. Bob and Lou hosted a $100-a-plate fundraising dinner for Funston at their Nichols Hills home. After Funston was defeated in the primary, Bob threw his support behind the eventual winner, George Nigh.

During 1978, many leading Democrats looked to Bob to fill the United States Senate seat being vacated by Henry Bellmon in 1980. Bob considered his options. He was extremely busy boosting the development of a statewide water plan and was a partner and shareholder in the Oklahoma City law firm of Kerr, Irvine & Rhodes. The firm originally was organized as Kerr, Conn and

Davis in 1953 with RSK as the senior partner. However, Bob, Francis S. Irvine, and Horace G. Rhodes reorganized the firm.[1]

In addition to his law practice, Bob, at age 52, served as a director of Kerr-McGee Corporation and Fidelity Bank, N.A. He also was chief executive officer and chief financial officer of the Kerr Foundation and served on the managing boards of a dozen civic, charitable, and educational groups, including the United Way, Salvation Army, and the Oklahoma City Chamber of Commerce.

Remembering his father's admonition to give back to his state and community when he could, Bob decided to be a candidate for the Democratic nomination for the United States Senate. He was already on the road much of the time talking about water and his possible candidacy. His old friends strongly urged him to make the race, as did many new friends he made at appearances from Broken Bow to Guymon.

Ending all speculation, Bob formally announced his candidacy for the Senate on April 16, 1979. He made the announcement first in his hometown of Ada, then moved on to news conferences in Oklahoma City and Tulsa. The theme of his announcement was that he should be known in his own right, not as the son of the late Robert S. Kerr. Bob told reporters, "For the past 15 years, I have been actively engaged voluntarily in public service in our state and nation, primarily in the fields of water resource development, education, agricultural development, the problems of our senior citizens, and community and economic development."[2]

For the next year, Bob talked about the issues, but declined to officially campaign for the Senate seat. He visited 200 cities and towns with the message that he opposed any tax increases or cuts in programs for the elderly and that he would continue to work for a statewide water plan.

LEFT: A Bob Kerr for U.S. Senate lapel sticker.

RIGHT: Bob announces his candidacy for the United States Senate in April, 1979. *Courtesy Oklahoma Publishing Company.*

RIGHT: Campaign workers were asked to do all sorts of things. Lou, right, and Fran Alexander sweep out the Kerr for Senate campaign headquarters in Oklahoma City.

By the time Bob began his official election campaign in May, 1980, the Democratic field was full. Other candidates announcing their intentions to run included State Senate President Pro Tempore Gene Howard of Tulsa, former Senate President Pro Tempore James "Jim" Hamilton of Poteau, Oklahoma County District Attorney Andrew M. "Andy" Coats, and John Zelnick of Broken Arrow. Early announced Republican candidates were Tulsa industrialist John Zink, freshman State Senator Don Nickles of Ponca City, and Billy Joe Clegg of Oklahoma City, who had run unsuccessfully for various offices as an independent. Also considering the race were James Inhofe of Tulsa and University of Oklahoma president William Banowski.

On May 18, Bob opened his state campaign headquarters at 2307 Classen Boulevard in Oklahoma City. Later that day, he kicked off his campaign by appearing at a noon rally at the Kerr Center on the campus of East Central State University in Ada and at a rally that night in Muskogee's Downtown Civic Center.[3]

By filing day in July, 20 candidates paid the necessary fees to compete for Bellmon's Senate seat. Eleven Democrats and five Republicans tossed their hats into the ring for their respective party's nomination. In addition to the previously announced candidates of Bob, Hamilton, Coats, Howard, and Zelnick, more Democrats joined the race. They included former Judge Gar Graham of Oklahoma City, Oklahoma City businessman Gil Burk, Johnny Borders, Richard W. Klabzuba, Howard W. Joplin of McAlester, and Paul English, newspaper reporter and president of the Oklahoma City school board.

Joining Zink, Nickles, and Clegg on the GOP primary slate were Thorne Stallings and Ed Noble, a Tulsan and member of the family of famous Oklahoma philanthropists. Two Libertarian Party candidates filed, Loren Baker, an Oklahoma City attorney, and Robert Murphy, a Tulsa businessmen. Also, former Democratic attorney general and corporation commissioner, Charles Nesbitt, and Paul E. Trent filed as independent candidates in the crowded field.

Ronn Cupp took a leave of absence from OWI and OWDF to be Bob's traveling aide during the campaign. They traveled to every county in the state. Bob was a hard working but somewhat reluctant campaigner. Cupp joined a staff of more senior campaigners such as Mike Kelly, Bill Crain, Richard Mildren, and Mike Clingman.

Bob acquired a 1965 Beechcraft Queen Air for the campaign. The airplane made it much easier to cover the vast expanse of Oklahoma. Cupp was so accustomed to flying to destinations, and hearing the "clunk" when the landing gear fell into place, he was taken aback one day in the Panhandle when he did not hear the familiar sound. Suddenly, the pilot began to climb and later admitted sheepishly that he had failed to lower the landing gear. Bob was asleep and never knew about the close call.

On another occasion, the campaign schedule called for Bob and Cupp to appear in a parade in Oologah on a Sunday. They thought it strange for a parade to be on Sunday, but traveled to Oologah anyway. There was no parade—it had occurred the previous day.

Bob headed into the hot summer months toward the primary election on August 26. Former House Speaker Carl Albert was named honorary chairman of the campaign. Albert said he supported Bob because of his past service in education, health care, and natural resources development. Albert said, "Bob Kerr, Jr. will be a strong and effective voice for Oklahoma in the U.S. Senate."[4]

"I want to meet, talk with, and listen to as many Oklahomans as I possibly can," was Bob's goal during the home stretch of the

RIGHT: Bob, right, shakes hands with a supporter at a campaign rally. *Courtesy Oklahoma Publishing Company.*

BELOW: Bob rides in the back of a pickup truck in one of dozens of parades on the 1980 campaign trail.

race. He called for "a realistic set of energy priorities" at the federal level. He said he supported pending legislation that would exempt a royalty owner's first 10 barrels of daily production from the windfall profits tax, a congressionally-imposed tax he labeled as "unfair" to small interest owners. He estimated the proposed federal law would exempt up to 75 percent of Oklahoma's royalty owners from the tax. Most of the two to three million royalty owners in the United States were small farmers, ranchers, and elderly people who needed their royalty checks to provide for necessities.[5]

Lou and the Kerr children also took the campaign trail to the grassroots. Kerr-A-Vans traveled more than 4,000 miles to 120 cities and towns, taking the message that Bob was the right candidate to send to Washington.

Bob developed a strong network of friends and supporters in each of the state's 77 counties. For example, in Seminole County, former Seminole Mayor Melvin Moran was county chairman of the Kerr campaign. He remembered, "It was easy being for Bob. He was well qualified, was a good campaigner, and identified with people."[6]

At nearly every stop on the campaign trail, Bob had to fight complacency. People would tell him that they knew his father or that he should win going away. Bob always responded by say-

Bob and Lou at the watch party in the August, 1980, primary. Bob led the field of candidates by a small margin. *Courtesy Oklahoma Publishing Company.*

ing he needed voters' help and that nothing could be taken for granted.

When criticized by other candidates for supporting transfer of eastern Oklahoma's surplus water, Bob was forced to hold a news conference to clarify his position. When opponents charged he wanted to send water to western Oklahoma without thinking of the needs of heavily Democratic eastern Oklahoma, Bob responded, "We have surplus water in eastern Oklahoma, but I will never support the transfer of water which is needed in the area of origin for present needs and future growth."[7]

In late July, three weeks before the primary, a pollster hired by candidate Gene Howard found Bob leading the pack. Richard Morris of Dresner, Morris and Tororello, a New Jersey political consulting firm, said a poll of 500 persons showed Bob with 31 percent, Howard and Coats each with 17 percent, and Hamilton with 7 percent. The rest were undecided. Morris concluded there would be a Democratic runoff and that Bob would "definitely be in it."[8]

Coats made Bob's water transfer plan a major issue in the campaign. Coats said, "It was hard for me to oppose water transfer because my family roots on my mother's side were deep in the soil of western Oklahoma. However, it seemed to me that water transfer would be terribly expensive and probably cost prohibitive."[9]

Coats' views on water transfer were not well received in places such as Altus where he was soundly booed. "But they did play well in eastern Oklahoma," Coats remembered, "where people were concerned that water transfer would dry up their lakes and rivers."[10]

The Coats' candidacy gained ground on Bob in the final two weeks of the primary contest. When the votes were counted on August 26, Bob led the field, but not by much. His lead was less than 2,000 votes over Coats, 156,666 to 154,762. Gene Howard was a distant third, garnering slightly more than 55,000 votes. Hamilton ran fourth, another 5,000 votes behind.[11] Ronn Cupp blamed the disappointing showing on the failure of Bob's supporters to go to the polls. Previous polling data had shown Bob with a strong lead in areas where less than 25 percent of the registered Democrats voted.

Coats carried Oklahoma County impressively, 31,780 to 14,919, although Bob expected his nearest opponent to do even better in his home county. In Tulsa County, Bob led Coats 15,536 to 11,548. Howard only received 9,325 votes in his home county.[12]

On the Republican side, Nickles led Zink by less than 2,000 votes, forcing a runoff.[13]

Bob and Coats came out swinging for the three-week runoff campaign scheduled for September 16. Bob accused Coats of "playing fast and loose with the truth" during the campaign. He said Coats had falsely accused him of supporting the federal windfall profits tax.[14]

Coats, who had resigned as district attorney in Oklahoma City to run for the Senate, responded with his own charges that Bob avoided taking stands on issues when he declined to appear with other candidates in a televised debate.[15]

Coats was worried by Bob's move of bringing in political professionals to set up phone banks that allowed his recorded personal message to be sent to voters in every precinct of the state. Coats sent one of his people to observe the phone bank operation. Coats said, "She came back telling us that the Kerr phone banks were working so well and they were enlisting so many volunteers that she did not see how we could possibly win."[16]

Even though Bob Kerr Sr. had been dead for 17 years, voters did not realize it. When Coats shook hands with an older lady in Poteau and told her he was running for the United States Senate against Bob Kerr, the lady thought about it a minute and said, "I think I'll vote for you. I believe he's been in there long enough."[17]

Frankly, the Kerr name provided one disadvantage for Bob's candidacy. People knew that the Kerr family had extensive wealth and some were reluctant to contribute money to the campaign, although Bob was clearly the leading candidate.[18]

Water development became an issue in the runoff. There was no doubt where Bob stood on creation of a statewide water transfer system. Coats came out against the plan, although he said he was interested in looking at future water transfer plans.[19]

Another issue was whether or not the Democratic Senate hopefuls would support the party's presidential nominee against Republican Ronald Reagan in the 1980 presidential race. Bob, a loyal, lifelong Democrat, had no hesitancy about supporting the reelection of President Carter, even though he was disappointed in Carter's handling of water policy. Coats, on the other hand, tried to distance himself from the presidential race which Reagan was expected to win handily in Oklahoma.

In two television debates, it was obvious that Bob and Coats agreed on most issues. Both wanted a strong defense, a balanced budget, repeal of the windfall profits tax on oil, and less government spending.

"There wasn't much in the way of oratorical fireworks," Coats remembered 25 years later, "because neither of us said anything bad about the other, a far cry from today's ugly political mud slinging fests." During the campaign, when Coats was asked about Bob's ability, he said his opponent was a fine man and would do a good job for Oklahoma. However, Coats told audiences that he, as a courtroom-trained advocate, would be more effective in representing Oklahoma on the floor of the United States Senate.[20]

The amicable relationship between Coats and Bob carried over to their campaign staffs. Coats' strategists, Charlie Swinton and Larry Joplin, relative newcomers to running political campaigns, were trying to develop a plan to sweep their candidate to victory in the race for the Democratic nomination. Swinton had worked as a volunteer in the former campaigns of David Hall and Larry Derryberry, and Joplin was a Coats' employee in the district attorney's office.

Joplin, now a judge on the Oklahoma Court of Civil Appeals, remembered, "Andy had a great deal of admiration and appreciation for what the entire Kerr family had done for Oklahoma. In addition, he was genuinely fond of Bob. Even though both sides were working constantly to defeat the other, on those occasions when we would be together, it was very enjoyable. We shared a camaraderie with Mike Kelly, Bill Crain, and Richard Mildren."[21]

The week before the election, Bob took his campaign to his birthplace of Ada where he had finished second to Coats in Pontotoc County balloting in the primary. As Bob walked into a senior citizens nutritional center, a woman shook his hand, recalled his father, RSK, and said, "You look like him, too!"

Bob took advantage of the link with the town where he had lived until the second grade. He told a group of supporters that Ada was his emotional home. He said, "Every time I come down here, it's a sentimental journey. I had my first date here, and I learned to drive a car here."[22]

Hugh Warren, an Ada car dealer and Bob's local campaign manager, apologized to the crowd that the county had "gone to Coats." Warren said, "We just didn't think we'd have to worry here." Ada druggist, Billy Bryan, a former RSK campaign coordinator, introduced Bob to the crowd, "We can all remember what Bob Sr. did for us and Bob has deep roots here too."[23]

From Ada, Bob flew to Tulsa where he again attacked the windfall profits tax on oil and gas royalties and said he would play a leading role in Washington as an advocate for the elderly. "Those citizens most responsible for helping build our American dream," he said, "must not be forced into an economic nightmare created by the federal government's insensitivity and bureaucratic bungling."24

Campaigning in Lawton, Bob picked up the support of Representative Roy Hooper, Jr., a member of the legislature's joint Special Committee on Water Development. Hooper told supporters at a rally, "Bob is the only candidate who fully understands the vital importance of water to the economic and personal growth of both our rural and urban areas."25

Two days before the September 16 election, John Greiner, a reporter for *The Daily Oklahoman*, wrote an analysis of the Kerr-Coats race. He had spent time on the campaign trail with Bob, who was concerned that his supporters had been apathetic in the primary because the press had reported for months that he was the frontrunner. About the runoff, Bob said, "The apathy is gone, and my organization is intent in getting our supporters to the polls on election day."26

Even before the final results of the balloting on September 16 were made public, Bob knew he was not winning enough votes in the state's two largest counties, Oklahoma and Tulsa, to beat Coats. The final tally gave Coats a victory margin of slightly more than 24,000 votes, 209,952 to 185,814.27

At 10: 30 p.m., Bob stood with wife, Lou, at the podium in the ballroom at the Hilton Inn West Hotel in Oklahoma City and conceded to Coats, whom he promised to vigorously support in the general election.

Fifteen minutes after Bob's concession speech, Coats thanked him publicly for his support against Nickles, who easily defeated

206 MR. WATER: ROBERT S. KERR, JR.

LEFT: Bob emerges from the voting booth after casting his ballot in the runoff election on September 16, 1980. *Courtesy Oklahoma Publishing Company.*

BELOW: Bob, left, at an Oklahoma City rally for Gary Hart's bid for the presidency in 1984. *Courtesy Oklahoma Publishing Company.*

Zink for the Republican nomination. Coats called Bob "a gentleman."28

Two months later, in the general election, Nickles, on the coattails of a huge Reagan landslide in Oklahoma, beat Coats by more than 100,000 votes. As Coats later said, "That year, any Republican would have beaten any Democrat."29 The Republican landslide also help defeat RSK III in his bid for reelection to the Oklahoma House of Representatives. However, RSK II was elected lieutenant governor of Oklahoma in 1986.

Bob and Coats remained friends after the election. In the weeks and months that followed, they often met and shook their heads over all that had occurred. Coats said, "I think he was genuinely sorry I had not been elected."30

An important footnote to the election occurred 20 years later when Coats, who had become dean of the University of Oklahoma School of Law, lunched with Bob to explain a capital campaign to build a major addition to the law school. Coats said, "Bob and his brother, Bill, both graduates of the law school, were kind and generous enough to make a substantial gift, enabling us to build the student lounge and quiet study area which has been named in his honor."31

With the 1980 Senate race behind him, Bob moved on. He still believed he could make a difference in the state's future by continuing the fight for a comprehensive water plan.

Lou and Bob hosted a party at their home preceding a benefit concert for the Women's Auxiliary of the Salvation Army. At left are Major Ralph Morrell and Mrs. Morrell of the Salvation Army. *Courtesy Oklahoma Publishing Company.*

THE 1980 WATER PLAN

> *Those who refuse to face the reality of Oklahoma's increasing need for water for the entire state emulate the proverbial ostrich whose head goes into the sand at the first sign of danger.*
>
> —Robert S. Kerr, Jr.
>
> *Dad's effort in selling Oklahomans on a comprehensive water plan was much more difficult than his father's successful promotion of the Arkansas River Navigation Project. People could see a port and barges moving goods—they could not visualize the importance of moving water from east to west.*
>
> —Robert S. Kerr III
>
> *Bob Kerr, Jr. was the only person who could bring the competing and often divisive interests of eastern and western Oklahoma together to support a comprehensive water plan. His integrity and water development savvy made people listen to his well reasoned plans. He had a political and pragmatic vision that no one else had.*
>
> —Herschal Crow

Much was accomplished by Bob and Oklahoma Water, Inc. in the decade of the 1970s. As the most public water development organization in the state, OWI looked back at successful support for construction funding of Arcadia Lake and McGee Creek Reservoirs in Oklahoma. OWI continued to educate the next generation by sponsoring a state-wide conservation and development essay contest.

The essay topic in 1980 was, "What optimal water conservation and development will do for Oklahoma?" High school students filled in the names of their hometowns and submitted an essay in competition for cash prizes and commemorative bronze medallions in recognition of the opening of the McClellan-Kerr Navigation System. Winners were also awarded field trips of the navigation system.

In 1979, the legislature passed Senate Bill 215, the Water Development Financial Assistance Program, which allowed the Oklahoma Water Resources Board to sell investment certificates to fund many necessary water development projects across the state, and in some cases, even make grants-in-aid. After a court fight, the OWRB was able in 1980 to begin processing requests for assistance under the new program.

The most significant event in water development in 1980 was OWRB's release of the final two-phase draft of the state comprehensive water plan (Water Plan). The state had been mandated by the legislature 17 years before to develop such a plan, spurred by the 1966 Bureau of Reclamation survey titled, "Water, the Key to Oklahoma's Future," that really started the controversy about the transfer of water. Through battles in the public arena and in legislative conference rooms, the OWRB report made its way to the light of day.

Because 1980 was an election year, legislative leaders chose to defer a vote on the Water Plan until the new legislature would convene in January, 1981. Throughout 1979 and 1980, RSK III, as chairman of a joint legislative committee charged with writing the Water Plan, held public hearings in all sections of the state, seeking input from citizens. When RSK III was defeated in the 1980 election, Lawton State Representative Roy Hooper, Jr., took control of the legislation in the House of Representatives.

The Water Plan was an ambitious proposal that would provide additional water to Oklahoma's parched west and southwest by transferring surplus water from the substantial reservoirs in the eastern part of the state. The plan was to be accomplished by transferring water by separate northern and southern conveyance systems, strikingly similar to a proposal made 15 years before by Bob and other water transfer advocates and government agencies.

The 1980 Water Plan presented a long-range, flexible strategy for managing and developing Oklahoma's water resources through 2040. It included suggestions on how to meet future requirements of cities and towns for industrial and residential water consumption.

The most significant part of the Water Plan was to provide a permanent mechanism to finance community water and sewer system improvements. The Statewide Water Development Revolving Fund (SWDRF) was funded by the legislature two years later with $25 million in seed money. The main purpose of the SWDRF was to serve as collateral for revenue bonds issued by the OWRB. Loan money was generated through the sale of bonds. The proceeds were then loaned to eligible applicants who repaid principal and interest over an extended period of time. Grant funds were also made available for emergency water and sewer problems.[1]

It took two attempts to amend Oklahoma's lengthy constitution to allow the SWDRF to function. In addition to Bob, Glenn Sullivan, Ronn Cupp, and Ed Pugh of Governor George Nigh's office were instrumental in convincing Oklahomans to pass the constitutional amendments.

Robert S. Kerr III believes the section of the Water Plan that allowed local cities and towns to develop water resources is the most significant and unrecognized economic development legislation in the history of Oklahoma. He said, "You can look at an Oklahoma map and count dozens of cities that have upgraded water and sewer facilities only because SWDRF was available to them. The new funding mechanism gave cities and towns the means to survive economically and attract much needed industrial development."[2]

Governor Nigh hosted the state's largest-ever water meeting in December, 1980. More than 800 people attended the conference in Oklahoma City. Bob, as conference chairman, opened the meeting with a stirring speech about the importance of water development. He said:

> The conservation and development of our water resources represents the single greatest challenge for Oklahomans during the next decade. The topics we will discuss here today—energy, agriculture, industry, and the environment—are all part of that challenge, and must be addressed in our comprehensive water plan.
>
> So, it is appropriate that we meet here today at the beginning of a new decade to reason, to discuss, to debate once again the issue which has so often in the past felt the sting of debate. It is my hope that the "issue of the 80s" will become our "challenge of the 80s," and that we will accept the challenge to conserve and develop Oklahoma's water resources not only for our own benefit, but for the benefit of future generations of Oklahomans to come.[3]

The Governor's Water Conference, at Oklahoma City's Sheraton Century Center, presented a number of experts, including Herbert Grubb, director of planning for the Texas Department of Water; Bill Gamel, chief of engineering for the Tulsa District of the Corps of Engineers; and James Barnett, executive director of the OWRB.

Joe Hall, conservation officer for the Western Area Power Administration, was one of several nationally recognized water experts to address the conference and chide Oklahomans for delaying decisions on water transfer. Hall said state and federal agencies were negligent in waiting on each other to take the lead in getting a water transfer plan moving.[4]

Governor Nigh, as the keynote speaker, predicted water would replace energy in the decade ahead as the foremost challenge of the state.

With interest in water development seeming at an all-time high, Bob dug in his heels and called his troops to action. On January 12, 1981, he wrote OWI members, "It is now apparent that we need to capture the impetus gained from the governor's water meeting before it is lost."[5]

Bob convened a meeting of key individuals from agriculture, business, and government sectors to discuss and develop a plan to convince the legislature to approve the Oklahoma Comprehensive Water Plan. In sounding the call for the legislature to act, Bob said:

> If last summer's debilitating drought told us anything, it is that we can no longer sit idly by, blinded by parochial interest, and expect Oklahoma's water problems to be solved on a piecemeal basis. It's time for us to get together to assure the development, passage, and completion of a statewide water plan. Our roads and highways are constructed and maintained with a combination of county, state, and federal funds. How much more important is an adequate water supply?

The Oklahoma legislature finally approved the Water Plan. In the gallery during final debate of the bill in the House of Representatives were Bob and RSK III, who was disappointed he was not on the House floor leading the fight for the Water Plan.

When RSK III expressed his disappointment to his father, Bob turned to him and said, "Don't be disappointed. No one can take from you all the work you have accomplished to push the Water Plan through the legislature." Again, Bob saw the big picture. He told his son, "All that matters is that we have a Water Plan for the first time in state history."[6]

Legislative approval of the Water Plan was an empty victory as far as water transfer was concerned. Ultimately, the water transfer components of the 1980 Water Plan were found to be economically not feasible under federal guidelines. Even though many leaders believed the 1980 plan was the answer to solving Oklahoma's future water needs, the state could never realistically fund the construction of the conveyance system with its own money. Because the water transfer project could not be justified under federal guidelines, federal money was not available. Thus, for the near future, the idea of water transfer was dead.

However, the 1980 Water Plan did lay the groundwork for the Oklahoma legislature to adopt many changes in water development. Statewide floodplain management legislation ensured every Oklahoma town had access to affordable flood insurance. The OWRB assisted city and county officials in implementing sound management programs aimed at guiding development in flood-prone areas, thereby mitigating future flood losses. By 2005, nearly 400 Oklahoma cities and counties had participated in the National Flood Insurance Program administered by the OWRB.[7]

Another recommendation of the 1980 Water Plan was for state support of the Red River Chloride Control Project, an effort which Bob and OWI had backed for years. The Corps of Engineers project was aimed at combating the natural salt pollution in the Red River, which made water from the river virtually unusable for irrigation or municipal or industrial water supplies.

The Corps's initial pilot project, across the Red River border in Texas, was successful, removing nearly 90 percent of the chlorides contributed by the South Fork of the Wichita River. The idea was to bypass 10 major salt sources in southwest Oklahoma and northwest Texas.

Weather modification also gained momentum in the 1980 Water Plan. The OWRB was given regulatory control over cloud seeding operations. The Plan also encouraged scientific research and development of weather modification strategies.[8]

In 1982, Governor Nigh appointed Bob as a member of the Oklahoma Water Resources Board. OWRB executive director James "Jim" Barnett, who had served as legal counsel to the board before being named director in 1979, said, "Bob was an incredible asset on the Water Resources Board. He had the background, and people respected him. He understood that as a member of the board, he could not micromanage the staff. He understood his role very well and helped set policy for the future."[9]

Patty Eaton, who served with Bob on the Oklahoma Water Resources Board, said, "He was so valuable to the board. He always knew the background of every water problem that we considered. He had lived Oklahoma water development for most of his life."[10]

Bob and Lou began spending more time at the family compound in Minnesota in the 1980s. The compound had become legendary for family gatherings. It provided opportunities for cousins such as Bob and Aubrey Kerr to renew close ties that had begun at Grandma Kerr's house in Ada years before.

RIGHT: Bob, standing, and Lou hosted a party for artist Enoch Kelly Haney, left. Seated beside Haney are Sherry and Breene Kerr. *Courtesy Oklahoma Publishing Company.*

BELOW: Bob, left, demonstrates his outdoor cooking talents to Mary Anna d'Andriole, center, and Beverly Cox. Bob acted as brisket chef for a patrons party for Allied Arts. *Courtesy Oklahoma Publishing Company.*

ABOVE: Left to right, George Swisher, Ginny Swisher, Lou, and Bob at a charity event hosted by the Kerrs. *Courtesy Oklahoma Publishing Company.*

RIGHT: Bob, right, and other members of the Kerr-McGee Corporation board of directors and management team inspect a Kerr-McGee coal mine in Wyoming. *Courtesy Kerr-McGee Corporation.*

Aubrey remembered sitting for hours, just talking to Bob, "Our relationship was special, an unusual closeness for cousins. We could talk for hours without really saying much. We shared family experiences that were unforgettable. And sometimes we just sat there. A lot passed between us without words."11

Bob's role as a director of Kerr-McGee Corporation took on added significance in the early 1980s when a decade-long oil boom became a bust. The active drilling rig count, an indicator of oil and gas activity in several states, was at an all-time high in Oklahoma in 1982. Sales records at Rolls Royce and Mercedes-Benz dealers were broken monthly. Bankers and investors were so excited about putting their money into the oil patch that Penn Square Bank, located in a shopping center in northwest Oklahoma City, became an icon of the exuberance and careless banking practices that beset oil-hungry banks.[12]

A sustained drop in energy prices and resulting bankruptcies in the petroleum industry caused Penn Square Bank to fail. In domino fashion, larger banks folded. Falling oil prices had a catastrophic effect upon the budgets of oil-producing states such as Oklahoma and adversely affected the operations of energy giants such as Kerr-McGee.

Frank McPherson became chief executive officer of the company in 1983. "For awhile," he said, "there was a question whether we could survive."[13] McPherson had to make tough calls to restructure Kerr-McGee to keep it alive.

Bob spent many hours during the dark days of the oil bust at Kerr-McGee headquarters. McPherson remembered, "He was very, very supportive as a director. I could always count on Bob to be straightforward with his questions and comments."[14]

Bob was supportive of McPherson's efforts to literally change the face of Kerr-McGee. Its longtime uranium business was shut down. Other assets were peeled off to make the company lean and profitable. McPherson said, "I always knew that if I laid out the strategy in a sound business plan, and told him my reasons, Bob would support me fully. He never once disappointed me."[15]

Besides being a veteran, astute Kerr-McGee director, Bob was a personal encouraging factor for McPherson. "Bob was a gentle man of great integrity and of the highest principles. It meant so much to me when he would pull me aside after a board meeting and say, 'Frank, you're doing a good job, and I just want to encourage you to keep it up."[16]

Kerr-McGee became an international company in the 1980s. For decades, the company had dabbled in worldwide properties, but truly became a major international player in the oil and gas industry after the oil bust loosened its grip on the national economy.[17]

In 1984, State Senators Rodger Randle and Penny Williams of Tulsa appointed Bob to a citizen-legislator committee to oversee the Oklahoma Tax Commission's development of new standards for county assessors.[18]

The goal was for the assessor in each of the state's 77 counties to assess property for ad valorem tax purposes in the same way. History had shown that assessment varied greatly county by county. Bob was joined on the committee by former Governor and United States Senator Henry Bellmon.

Also in 1984, Bob was involved in the merger of the holding company of Fidelity Bank in Oklahoma City with BancOklahoma in Tulsa. Fidelity Bank, one of the state's oldest banks, organized in 1908, was the fifth largest banking institution in Oklahoma. The Bank of Oklahoma was the third largest bank in the state. Bob, as a director of Fidelity of Oklahoma, Inc., approved of the merger, making the Bank of Oklahoma a truly statewide bank with $3 billion in assets.[19]

Bob and his brother, Bill, had been major shareholders of Fidelity Bank for years. So had Dean A. McGee and James J. Kelly, retired president of Kerr-McGee. The merger combined not only large banks, but principal commercial interests in the state. BancOklahoma was closely connected with the Williams Companies in Tulsa, one of that city's major corporations.[20]

Bob worked long hours as a member of the Goals for Central Oklahoma Council, a group that platted the future of the Oklahoma City Chamber of Commerce. In anticipation of the centennial of the land run of 1889 that opened what became Oklahoma City and most of central Oklahoma for settlement, the committee advanced plans for adding new water resources for central Oklahoma, expanding highway systems, studying mass transportation ideas, solving environmental problems, revamping the downtown area, and improving housing and living conditions.[21]

Working with Bob for a quarter century on Oklahoma City Chamber of Commerce projects was government relations vice president Dean Schirf, who said, "It was always good to

Left to right, Kay Kerr Adair, Margaret "Moni" Kerr Boylan, and Jewell Kerr.

have Bob on your team, as your chances to achieve the objective improved. He was a man of presence, substance, and quiet dignity that followed him everywhere he went."22

LEFT: Lillie Campbell was a longtime assistant to the Kerr family. She traveled with the family and oversaw household duties from 1959 to 2002.

BELOW: In 1986, Bob and Lou were in a reception line to meet Queen Elizabeth II of Great Britain.

Shari Kerr, right, and daughter, Katie.

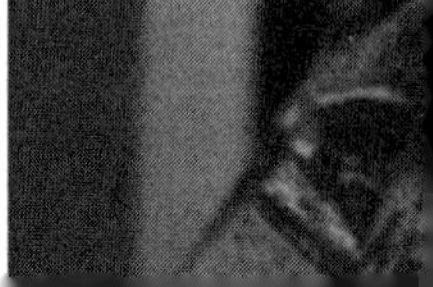

LEFT: The Kerr cousins during a visit in Minnesota at the home of Aubrey and Nancy Kerr. Left to right, Carole McClendon, Lou, Bob, Kay Kerr Adair, Ann Crawford, Bill Kerr, Nancy Kerr.

BELOW: Bob on one of his last visits to his beloved Northhome in Minnesota.

ABOVE: Left to right, Katie Kerr, Lou Kerr, Laura Lynn Kerr, Shari Kerr, Valerie Kerr, and Laura Kerr.

LEFT: Laura Dyanne Kerr.

228 MR. WATER: ROBERT S. KERR, JR.

ABOVE: Left to right, Jerrie Anderson, Brenda Knott, Jim Anderson, and Nancy Kerr.

LEFT: Left to right, Bob, Lou, Valerie Kerr Hart, and Dan Hart at Dan and Valerie's wedding.

LOWER LEFT: Bob and Valerie.

BELOW: The Kerr family gathered for the wedding of Mike and Nancy Kerr. Front row, left to right, Joffa Kerr, Lou Kerr, Nancy McClendon, Jewel Kerr, Nancy Kerr, Ann Crawford. Top row, Bill Kerr, Joe McClendon, Katie McClendon, Cody Kerr, Aubrey McClendon, Margaret Boylan, Mike Kerr, Nancy Landon Kerr, Aubrey Kerr, Shelley Kerr, Bob Kerr, Carolyn Kerr, Bill Crawford, Jerrie Anderson and Jim Anderson.

LEFT: Left to right, David Ogle, Laura Kerr Ogle, and Lou Kerr. In front, Taylor and Jackson Ogle.

AN ACTIVE ADVOCATE

BOB WAS KNOWN THROUGHOUT HIS LIFE for what jokingly was called the "Kerr Pause." Whether talking to business associates or family members, he used long

> *In times of turmoil, Bob always provided a steady hand. He always knew how to carefully approach any controversial subject and to do what was right.*
>
> —HORACE RHODES
>
> *Bob has been recognized as an Oklahoma Living Treasure for Tomorrow—and this he is, because he is always looking for the horizon of another day.*
>
> —WILLIAM J. VANDEN HEUVEL
>
> *He was bigger than life. In his disappointments, he would blame himself and not others. He did not believe in failure—they were just setbacks.*
>
> —LOU KERR

pauses to emphasize his admonitions. Longtime friend Richard "Dick" Poole explained the Kerr Pause, "Bob was a wise and thoughtful person. When making an observation or driving home a critical point, or answering an important question, he frequently employed long pauses to ensure that his comments were carefully crafted and precise. He never made offhand remarks that he would later regret."1

Poole, longtime vice president of Oklahoma State University, said, "Exploring ideas with this insightful man was a rewarding and beneficial experience."2 Even though Bob was humble and a real gentlemen during discussions of business or politics, he could be direct, forceful, and offer constructive criticism when circumstances so dictated.3

Bob had a great sense of history. He was devoted to his native Oklahoma and he and Lou were serious about their efforts to make Oklahoma a better place in which to live and work. Dick Poole reflected, "He always recognized the legacy of his father and what he, as the son of a legend, should give back to the state in the way of public service and commitment."4

Bob's commitment may have been best exemplified by his devotion and work as a trustee and later chairman of the Kerr Foundation. By 1984, the assets of the Kerr Foundation had grown to more than $71 million, multiplying by several times the worth of the foundation established by Grayce Kerr in 1963 following the death of her husband.

The four children of Bob Sr. had actively participated in the running of the foundation for two decades, but their interests were varied. When changing tax laws required a restructuring of the foundation, it was decided to split the assets into four institutions. The restructuring began in the middle of 1984 and was completed on January 1, 1985.

Larkin Warner, who directed the Economic Studies Division of the Kerr Foundation in the 1970s, described the four children of RSK, and their varied interests:

Each of the four siblings was truly brilliant. With their wide range of interests, they complemented each other. Breene was a hard-driving businessman with a wealth of innovative ideas and an outlook strongly influenced by his education and continued association with the Massachusetts Institute of Technology.

Bill was always ready with penetrating and often critical questions about proposed projects and exhibited an extensive knowledge of Oklahoma's political dynamics. Saintly Kay was concerned about using Foundation resources to help the needy. In some ways like Bob, Kay had a strong interest in protecting the environment. The four siblings truly respected and valued each other's opinions.[5]

Kay Kerr Adair's portion of the former Kerr Foundation assets went to the Kerr Center for Sustainable Agriculture (Kerr Center) headquartered at Poteau. That operation included the 4,000-acre experimental Kerr farm and ranch, now called the Stewardship Ranch. A research station at Vero Beach, Florida, was for many years part of the Kerr Center but became an independent nonprofit organization in 2004.

The Kerr Center produced a variety of educational activities, but its emphasis was on research and demonstration projects. In 2005, under the leadership of director, James "Jim" Horne, the Kerr Center continued to make grants for and fund both research and demonstration projects in farming/ranching technology. The goal is to encourage farmers to teach other farmers how to be more profitable, within a commitment to environmental sensitivity, social justice, and recovery of rural communities.

236 MR. WATER: ROBERT S. KERR, JR.

The Kerr clan gathered in Minnesota for the 1985 wedding of Billy and Laura Kerr. Front, left to right, Bob Adair, Kay Kerr Adair, Lou Kerr, Bob, Sam Kerr, Bill Kerr, Laura Kerr, LaMoyne Kerr, Jewel Kerr, Carole McClendon, Joe McClendon, Margaret Boylan, Lisa Boylan, and Lillie Campbell. Back row, Robert S. Kerr III, Kiersten Kerr, Charlotte Kerr, Steve Kerr, Beth Kerr, Laura Kerr, Valerie Kerr, Cody Kerr, Shari Kerr, Katie Kerr, Sandy Price, Christy Price, and Lori Clark.

AN ACTIVE ADVOCATE   237

In 1988, the Kerr Center acquired a century-old home in eastern Oklahoma and restored it to its original grandeur. The Overstreet-Kerr Historical Farm participates in a nationwide effort to preserve rare breeds of livestock and poultry. At the farm are displays of antique farm equipment, an orchard of heirloom varieties of fruit, and renovated outbuildings from the era in which the farm was built.[6]

RIGHT: Bob on a visit to Oklahoma State University in 1997 to observe research funded by a Kerr Foundation grant.

Breene Kerr established the Grayce B. Kerr Fund, which by 2005 had assets of more than $30 million, the 20th largest foundation in Maryland. Sheryl Kerr, the wife of Breene Kerr, was president of the foundation with headquarters in Easton, Maryland. In 2004, the fund announced a $1 million grant to Washington College.[7]

A separate Robert S. and Grayce B. Kerr Foundation was directed by Bill Kerr from his home in Jackson Hole, Wyoming. In 2005, that foundation was the third largest of its kind in Wyoming with assets of more than $34 million.[8]

Under the leadership of Bob and Lou, a new foundation, incorporated as The Kerr Foundation, Inc., quickly became one of Oklahoma's leading philanthropic funds. Its focus was to make grants in the areas of health, education, cultural development, and community service in Oklahoma, Arkansas, Colorado, Kansas, Missouri, New Mexico, Texas, and Washington, D.C.[9]

Lou had become a board member of the original Kerr Foundation in 1980. After the new foundation was created, she began active, daily involvement in foundation business. Because of her positive experience with early computers at her dress shop, Lou spearheaded efforts for the Kerr Foundation to employ cutting edge computer programs to track grants and produce cognitive and meaningful reports.[10]

Lou and Bob made a great team at the Kerr Foundation. She had creative ideas, and Bob was her sounding board. Lou said,

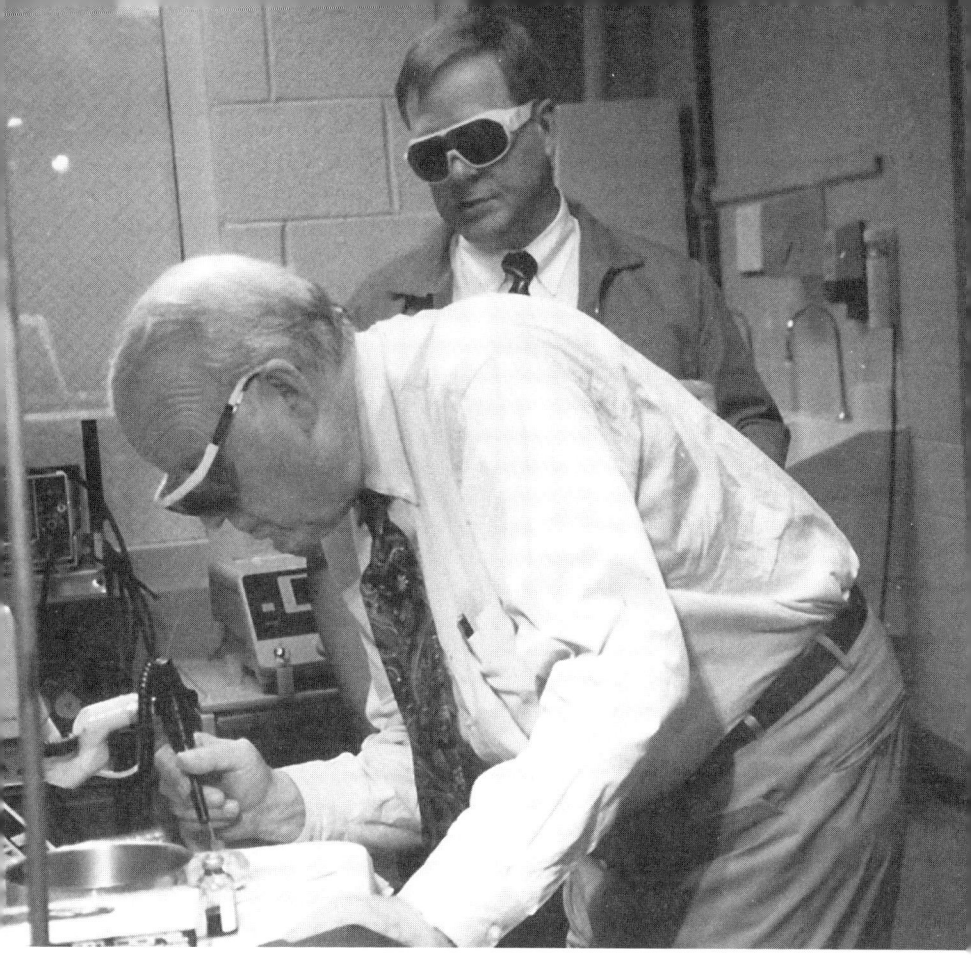

"He was a great listener. I would lay out the details of my idea and he would be the lawyer, throwing out 'what if' questions and giving me his advice on the value of the idea."[11] Often, after an idea was fully discussed, Bob would say, "OK, let's try it!"

Lou was a natural volunteer with an uncanny sense that allowed her to evaluate grant applications at the Kerr Foundation. She said, "I was a grant seeker long before I was a grant maker, and I think that made me a better grant maker. I see the mistakes of applying organizations because I have walked in those same steps." Lou developed forms and guidelines and ethics rules to assist nonprofit organizations.[12]

While Bob spent most of his time involved in water projects, Lou, for awhile as the only employee of the Kerr Foundation, to develop ombudsman and better health care programs for Oklahoma seniors. For years she had volunteered in Salvation Army projects, prompting Oklahoma Governor George Nigh to appoint her to a committee to write and evaluate senior-help programs.

The Kerr Foundation gave grants to the Salvation Army to buy buses to transport senior citizens from their homes to health care appointments and to the grocery store. Lou's theory was that activities for seniors would allow them to stay in their homes longer and reduce stays in hospitals or long-term care facilities.

Later in the administration of Governor Henry Bellmon, Lou lobbied for support of nutritional programs for seniors. Bellmon appointed her to a task force on nutrition.

Two of Bob's dogs, Brutus and Britney.

In its first 20 years, The Kerr Foundation, Inc. made nearly $30 million in grants to hundreds of organizations, primarily in Oklahoma. Grants were made to the National Cowboy Hall of Fame, the Tulsa Ballet Theatre, Red Earth, Oklahoma Arts Institute, the Oklahoma City Art Museum, many of the state's colleges and universities, the Oklahoma Educational Television Authority, the Nature Conservancy, the Oklahoma Centennial Commemoration Fund, Allied Arts Foundation, Dean A. McGee Eye Institute, Oklahoma Heritage Association, Oklahoma City National Memorial, and dozens of local school districts, hospitals, arts councils, and community groups.

Youth programs remain a priority for the Kerr Foundation, of which Lou assumed the presidency in 1999. Approximately 50 percent of the foundation's dollars go to education interests with the balance split among cultural, public service, and human service grants. In 2005, the Kerr Foundation, Inc. had assets of $28 million.

The foundation provides more than money to applicants. A staff of four assists Lou in getting involved with organizations that receive grants, helping with strategic planning, board building, and fundraiser event planning. It is the Kerr Foundation's goal that any recipient of a foundation grant succeeds as an independent entity.

In 1982, before the Kerr Foundation split into four separate funds, the ranch-style home of Bob and Grayce Kerr at the Poteau ranch was given to the State Regents for Higher Education. The 15,000-square-foot home became a "think tank" for state education leaders and private groups. Quickly, the Kerr Conference Center became a top regional conference center.

When Bob was not involved in Kerr Foundation activities, he still spent time with water issues. Although his dreams of a water transfer plan for Oklahoma had not been fulfilled, he continued his active participation in state and national water issues. He paid close attention to the Oklahoma Water Resources Board's monitoring of the state's water development.

For awhile, Bob served on the board of directors of Oklahoma Gas and Electric Company (OGE). He was helpful as a director and a hero to company president James Harlow. Bill Ross remembered, "Once when Jim had a real problem, he called Bob at midnight. Bob said, 'OK, shall I come over there, or do you want to come over here?'" After hours of discussion, Bob began calling other board members at daylight and solved the problem. By 7:00 a.m., the board was taking action on the emergency that blew over in a few days.[13]

Even though Bob was 63 as the 1990s began, it was an active decade for him. In addition to running the Kerr Foundation, and quoting Winston Churchill at breakfast with friends each morning, he was senior partner in the Oklahoma City law firm of Kerr, Irvine, Rhodes & Ables. The general practice firm, with expertise in administrative, agricultural, business, environmental, oil and gas, legislation, insurance defense, and water law, added six additional lawyers after Bob, Francis Irvine, and Horace Rhodes reorganized the firm in 1980.

The Kerr firm was loaded with experts in dealing with government agencies and insurance companies. Rhodes was a former deputy insurance commissioner and president of United Founders Life Insurance Company. The new lawyers were Angela Ables, James W. "Tad" Rhodes, James R. "Jim" Barnett, Jeff Hartmann, Robert A. Miller, and R. Thomas Lay.[14]

Ables was a former assistant attorney general and deputy insurance commissioner. Barnett joined the firm in 1991 after 19 years in state government, including a stint as general counsel and later executive director of the Oklahoma Water Resources Board. Lay was also a former Oklahoma assistant attorney general and general counsel of OWRB.

In 1989, while on a visit with son Bill in Phoenix, Arizona, Bob and Lou underwent what they thought were routine physical examinations at the Mayo Clinic branch in nearby Scottsdale. Lou's health was great, but doctors wanted to run additional tests on Bob.

Fortuitously, a University of Oklahoma-trained physician's assistant noticed something strange about Bob's lab results. A tiny elevation in one PSA test signaled the need for further diagnostic testing. Sure enough, the additional testing showed Bob had prostate cancer, but the disease was in its early stages and highly treatable.[15]

Mayo Clinic doctors prescribed medication for Bob. Downstairs, Lou expected to pay a few dollars for a 30-day supply of the medicine, but was shocked when the pharmacist at the clinic announced the cost was $550. She had to borrow money from Bob to pay for the prescription.[16]

The early diagnosis saved Bob's life. Medication shrank the cancerous tissue, and Bob was given a clean bill of health. He gave much credit for his extended life to God. Lou remembered, "He had a profound faith in God and a great appreciation of his surroundings. He always gave credit to God for his many blessings."[17]

Bob continued to serve on the boards of many organizations such as the Oklahoma United Methodist Church Foundation, the University of Oklahoma Board of Visitors, the University of Oklahoma Foundation, the National Academy of Public Administration, and the Committee for a Responsible Budget. He was president of Oklahoma 2000, a research affiliate of the Oklahoma State Chamber of Commerce and Industry.

Bob was an important member of the Board of Trustees of Oklahoma City University from 1987 to 1992. He and Lou contributed funds to establish the Robert S. Kerr, Jr. Distinguished Professorship at OCU. Bob was given an honorary doctor of law

letters degree from OCU in 1973 and was presented the OCU Distinguished Service Award in 1994.

Kerr-McGee Corporation, Bob, and his sister and brothers made possible the Robert S. Kerr, Jr. Chair in Natural Resources and Environmental Law at OCU. The family also funded the Robert S. Kerr, Sr. Chair in Constitutional Law at the university. The Kerr Foundation also gave the OCU School of Law $1.1 million for scholarships and faculty support and development.[18]

ABOVE: Bob, left, with Oklahoma City University President Dr. Jerald Walker, right, and his wife, Ginny. *Courtesy Oklahoma Publishing Company.*

RIGHT: Bob in front of his old room at the New Mexico Military Institute. He was inducted into the NMMI Hall of Fame in 1990.

When OCU president Dr. Jerald Walker announced plans in 1996 to cut the OCU School of Law's budget by $500,000, Dean Rennard Strickland objected and called Bob, who still retained the title as board member emeritus. The law school had been promised that its budget would not suffer because of the great amount of tuition from law students that went into the general fund of OCU.[19]

Dean Strickland was invited to meet with Bob at the Kerr Foundation offices on North May Avenue in Oklahoma City.

Bob told Strickland, "You know OCU is a religious institution and religious institutions cannot be about the business of doing one thing and saying another." Strickland agreed, but reminded Bob that President Walker was his boss.[20]

The following Monday morning, Bob accompanied Strickland to Walker's office. Bob told Walker, "You made an agreement with the law school and with Dean Strickland, and he relied upon that agreement in accepting the deanship." Bob said the Board of Trustees was aware of the agreement and would not go along with any recommendation to cut further into the law school budget.[21]

Strickland, whose budget remained intact, remembered, "I was so lucky to have a man of the integrity of Bob Kerr, Jr., who went to bat for the law school and expected the parties to keep their word and their obligations."[22]

In 2002, a major gift of the Kerr Foundation established an endowed chair at the Oklahoma Medical Research Foundation (OMRF). The Robert S. Kerr, Jr. Endowed Chair in Cancer Research became part of OMRF's internationally recognized immunobiology and cancer program. The Kerr gift allowed OMRF to bring another distinguished scientist to Oklahoma to learn how the immune system develops and how white blood cells turn into cancer cells.[23]

In April, 2003, Bob made a substantial gift to OMRF to establish Oklahoma's first endowed research chair targeting women's diseases. The Lou C. Kerr Endowed Chair in Biomedical Research will result in research focused on diseases and disorders afflicting women.[24]

Because he was a lifelong avid reader, it was a great heartbreak for Bob to lose much of his eyesight to macular degeneration. He spent much time at Johns Hopkins in Maryland and Dean A. McGee Eye Institute in Oklahoma City searching for answers. At McGee, Dr. David Parks tried to reverse the degeneration. John Jenson, a former professional baseball player attending the OCU School of Law, was hired as Bob's driver and reader. After Jenson graduated from law school, Dwayne Thornton, a retired Southwestern Bell Telephone Company executive, became Bob's daily companion.

Bob received Oklahoma's highest award in 2003 when he was inducted into the Oklahoma Hall of Fame, sponsored by the Oklahoma Heritage Association. Bob was part of a distin-

In 2000, Bob received the Treasures for Tomorrow Award. Left to right, Laura Kerr Ogle, Bob, Billy, Shari, and Cody Kerr.

guished class of inductees that included oil men Boone Pickens and William K. Warren, Jr., educator Dr. George Henderson, and William G. Paul, former president of the American Bar Association.

By the time of the Hall of Fame induction ceremony in Tulsa on November 20, 2003, Bob was weak from bone cancer that had wracked his body for more than a year. However, he stood tall to listen to his introduction by Ambassador William J. vanden Heuvel, who said, "Oklahoma's schools and colleges, its museums, and cultural centers know what Bob Kerr, Jr. has done for them as well as for those in need, the poor, the elderly, and the young citizens of this great state who have had his help and encouragement."[25]

Ambassador vanden Heuvel also said, "It is not only the generosity of Bob's philanthropy that sets him apart—the extraordinary mark of his life's work is the giving of himself, his time, his energy, his inspiration to so many."[26]

AN ACTIVE ADVOCATE   **247**

LEFT: Lou and Robert S. Kerr, IV, the son of Robert S. Kerr, III, known as "Sam Kerr." This photograph was taken at Sam's wedding.

RIGHT: James Austin Kerr, left, and Wilson Hixon Kerr, are the sons of Steve and Beth Kerr.

BELOW: : Katherine Lemoyne "Katie" Kerr, left, is Shari's daughter. At right is Kiersten Frances Kerr, the daughter of Robert S. Kerr, III.

RIGHT: Taylor Nicole Ogle is the daughter of David and Laura Kerr Ogle.

ABOVE: Elizabeth Kay Hart in 2004.

RIGHT: Mary Grayce Hart is the daughter of Dan and Valerie Kerr Hart.

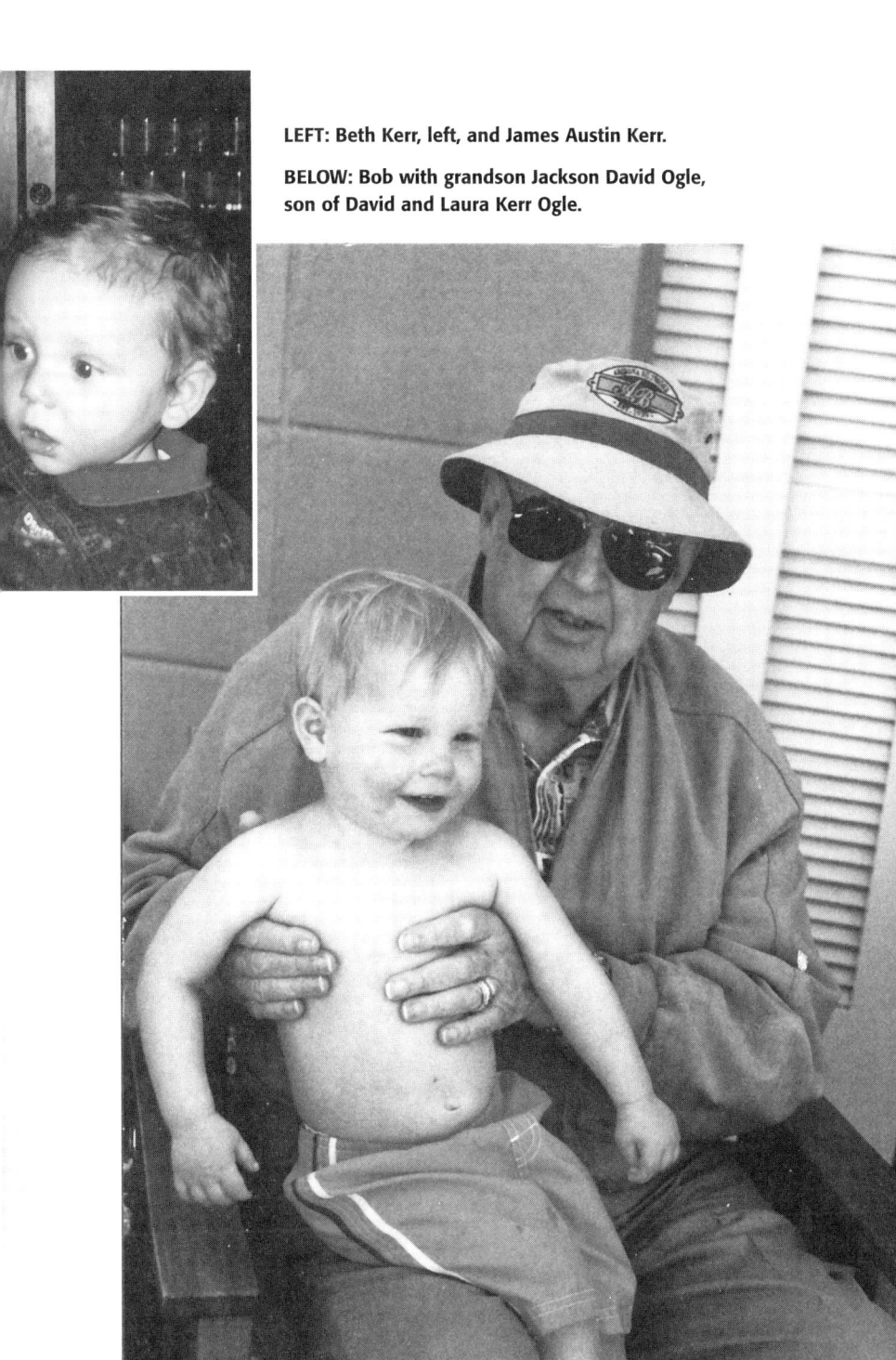

LEFT: Beth Kerr, left, and James Austin Kerr.

BELOW: Bob with grandson Jackson David Ogle, son of David and Laura Kerr Ogle.

ABOVE: University of Central Oklahoma President Roger Webb, left, joins Lou, Steve Kerr, and Laura Kerr Ogle at the dedication of the Kerr Lounge in UCO's Nigh University Center

LEFT: Bob and daughter, Shari.

In December, 2003, and January, 2004, Bob's condition worsened. The chemotherapy and pain associated with the advancing disease combined to prevent him from going to the office.

Bob and Lou with former Soviet President Mikal Gorbachev in October, 1997.

Just two months after his Hall of Fame induction, Bob, died, at age 77, on January 29, 2004. The caption for his photograph that appeared on the front page of *The Daily Oklahoman* was "A lifetime of community service."27

Luke Corbett, chairman and chief executive officer of Kerr-McGee Corporation, said, "The Kerr name is synonymous with leadership, generosity, and community support, and Robert S. Kerr, Jr. embodied all three. We value the service he provided our company for four decades as a member of the board of directors."28

Richard Mildren, an Oklahoma City attorney who had been Bob's scheduling assistant in the 1980 United States Senate race, told reporters, "He was a wonderful man and a credit to our state."29

The following week, a memorial service was held in the Bishop Angie Smith Chapel on the OCU campus. The Reverend

In 2002, a lounge honoring Bob was dedicated at the University of Oklahoma School of Law. Left to right, Shari Kerr, Brenda Knott, Billy Kerr, Bob, Lou, Steve Kerr, and Beth Kerr.

Grayson L. Lucky, pastor of Nichols Hills United Methodist Church, conducted the service that included words from Bishop Bruce P. Blake, head of the Oklahoma Conference of the United Methodist Church, The Reverend Daniel P. Junkin, and OCU President Tom McDaniel. Oklahoma-born opera star Leona Mitchell sang "The Lord's Prayer" and the OCU Choir performed "The Hallelujah Chorus" from Handel's "The Messiah." Dr. Rufus Fears, who had for years shared Bob's love for the clas-

sics, read one of Bob's favorite poems, "High Flight."[30]

After Bob's death, Lou reflected on their 32 years together, "Our love was a long and wonderful friendship that truly endured the space of time and tribulation. He loved his siblings and his children beyond measure."[31] The statewide audience watching the Hall of Fame broadcast in November, 2003, was reminded of the Kerr family philosophy of "putting something back in the pot." In the early days of the country, pioneers headed west, often on foot. As they traveled, people in settlements along the way would invite them to share food and spend the night. The next morning they went hunting. Before the visitor left on his way, he would leave a rabbit or squirrel in the pot to make up for what he had eaten.

"Put something back in the pot" was the guiding creed of Bob's life—and Oklahoma's pot is overflowing with his contributions.

LEFT: Bob's cousin and one of his lifetime best friends, Jim Anderson, visited Bob a few days before his death. For decades Bob had chided Jim for convincing him to attend military school in New Mexico. However, on the last visit, Bob whispered to Jim, "Thank you for the influence you had on my life."

BELOW: Bob and Lou had a wonderful 32 years of marriage before his death on January 29, 2004.

256   MR. WATER: ROBERT S. KERR, JR.

CHAPTER 1: A ROBUST ANCESTRY

1. James K. Anderson, *Tributaries and Rivulets: A Genealogic Review of My Anderson and Kerr Families* (Decorah, Iowa: Anundsen Publishing Company, 2000), p. 2, hereafter referred to as Kerr Family Genealogy.
2. Malvina Stephenson, *King of the Senate* (Tulsa, Oklahoma: Cock-A-Hoop Publishing, 1995), p. 2, hereafter referred to as *King of the Senate.*
3. Kerr Family Genealogy, p. K-1.
4. Ibid., K-2
5. *King of the Senate,* p. 2.
6. Ibid., p. 4.
7. Ibid., p. 6.
8. Ibidl. p. 8.
9. Ibid., p. 9.
10. Ibid., p. 11.
11. Ibid.
12. Ibid., p. 12.
13. Ibid.
14 Ibid.
15. Ibid., p. 13.
16. Ibid.
17. Ibid.
18. Ibid.
19. Ibid., p. 16.

CHAPTER 2: A LEGACY BEGINS

1. John Samuel Ezell, *Innovations in Energy: The Story of Kerr McGee* (Norman: University of Oklahoma Press, 1979), p. 8., hereafter referred to as *Innovations in Energy.*
2. Ibid., p. 9.
3. *King of the Senate,* p. 76.
4. Ibid., p. 78.
5. Ibid., p. 81.
6. Kerr Family Genealogy, p. K-60.
7. Interview with Breene Mitchell Kerr, January 13, 2004, hereafter referred to as Breene Kerr interview, Heritage Archives, Oklahoma City, Oklahoma, hereafter referred to as Heritage Archives.
8. Ibid.
9. Ibid.
10. Interview with Robert S. Kerr, Jr., in *Loon Songs,* edited by Kay Kerr Adair, January 10, 2003.
11. Ibid.
12. Ibid.
13. Breene Kerr interview.
14. Ibid., Kay Kerr Adair interview.
15. Kay Kerr Adair interview.
16. Interview with Robert S. Kerr, Jr., in *Loon Songs,* edited by Kay Kerr Adair, January 10, 2003.
17. *Loon Songs,* September 12, 2000.
18. Kay Kerr Adair interview.
19. Kerr Family Genealogy, p. K-58.
20. Interview with James K. "Jim" Anderson, December 15, 2004, hereafter referred to as Jim Anderson interview.
21. Kay Kerr Adair interview.

22. Kerr Family Genealogy, p. K-58.
23. Jim Anderson interview.
24. Ibid.
25. Interview with Margaret Kerr Boylan, April 15, 2005, Heritage Archives, hereafter referred to as Margaret Boylan interview.
26. Ibid.
27. Bob Burke and Louise Painter, *Justice Served: The Life of Alma Bell Wilson* (Oklahoma City: Oklahoma Heritage Association, 2001), p. 33-34.
28. Ibid., p. 40-41.
29. Jim Anderson interview.
30. www.nmmi.edu, official website of the New Mexico Military Institute.
31. Jim Anderson interview.
32. Ibid.
33. Ibid.
34. Ibid.
35. Interview with William Graycen Kerr, November 19, 2003, hereafter referred to as Bill Kerr interview, Heritage Archives.
36. Interview with Kay Kerr Adair, November 25, 2003, hereafter referred to as Kay Adair interview, Heritage Archives.
37. Ibid.
38. Bill Kerr interview.
39. Kay Adair interview.
40. Ibid.
41. *Innovations in Energy,* p. 38.

CHAPTER 3: LAND, WOOD, AND WATER
1. Robert S. Kerr, *Land, Wood & Water,* (New York: Fleet Publishing Corporation, 1960), p. 162, hereafter referred to as *Land, Wood & Water.*
2. Ibid., p. 166.
3. Ibid., p. 15.
4. Ibid., p. 33.
5. Ibid. p. 92.
6. Ibid. p. 95.
7. U.S. Army Corps of Engineers, *Water Resources Development by the U.S. Army Corps of Engineers in Oklahoma* (Tulsa, Oklahoma: 1977), p. 1, hereafter referred to as 1977 U.S. Army Corps of Engineers report.
8. Ibid., p. 2.
9. www.owrb.state.ok.us, official website of the Oklahoma Water Resources Board; Ann Hamilton, ed., *Oklahoma Almanac: 2003-2004* (Oklahoma City: Oklahoma Department of Libraries, 2003), p. 6.
10. Ibid., p. 7.
11. *Harlow's Weekly* (Oklahoma City, Oklahoma), October 27, 1923.
12. Ibid.
13. Ibid.
14. Reports of Oklahoma City Chamber of Commerce committees, Stanley Draper collection, Heritage Archives.
15. *Harlow's Weekly,* February 15, 1926.
16. *The Farmer-Stockman* (Oklahoma City, Oklahoma), January 21, 1926.
17. *The Daily Oklahoman* (Oklahoma City, Oklahoma), January 10, 1926.
18. *Harlow's Weekly,* January 15, 1926.
19. *Oklahoma* (Oklahoma City, Oklahoma), May 8, 1924.
20. Letter from Frank Buttram to Oklahoma City Chamber of Commerce, February 18, 1928, Heritage Archives.
21. Report of Oklahoma City Chamber of Commerce, December 10, 1927, Heritage Archives.
22. Letter from Stanley Draper to Loren A. Hutchins, December 23, 1927, Heritage Archives.
23. www.swt.usace.army.mil, the official website of the Tulsa District, U.S. Corps of Engineers.
24. *Land, Wood & Water,* p. 142.
25. Ibid., p. 109.
26. www.owrb.state.ok.us

CHAPTER 4: LEARNING THE ROPES
1. Press release from

Robert S. Kerr, March 25, 1954, Heritage Archives.
2. Interview with Robert S. Kerr, III, August 31, 2005, hereafter referred to as RSK III interview, Heritage Archives.
3. Interview with William "Bill" Ross, December 21, 2004, Heritage Archives.
4. LeRoy H. Fisher, ed. *Oklahoma's Governors, 1929-1955* (Oklahoma City: Oklahoma Historical Society, 1983), p. 143.
5 Kerr Foundation, Inc., Oklahoma City, Oklahoma, *The Waterway,* 1977, p. 29.
6 *Land, Wood, & Water,* p. 174.
7. Ibid., p. 175.
8. www.swt.usace.army.mil.
9. Ibid., p. 342.
10. Ibid., p. 177.
11. Ibid., p. 367.
12. A speech by Robert S. Kerr delivered at Oklahoma City, Oklahoma, November 9, 1945, Heritage Archives.
13. Ibid.
14. *The Daily Oklahoman,* June 3, 1962.
15. Ibid.
16. Ibid., January 2, 1963.
17. Ibid.

CHAPTER 5: BEARING THE BURDEN
1. Bill Kerr interview.
2. Martin Hauan, *He buys organs for churches,* pianos for bawdy houses (Oklahoma City: Midwest Political Publications, 1976), p. 180, hereafter referred to as Hauan, Organs and Pianos.
3. Hauan, *Organs and Pianos,* p. 184.
4. Bob Burke, *Good Guys Wear White Hats: The Life of George Nigh* (Oklahoma City: Oklahoma Heritage Association, 2000), p. 109, hereafter referred to as *Good Guys Wear White Hats*; Hauan, *Organs and Pianos,* p. 184.
5. *Good Guys Wear White Hats.,* p. 111.
6. Hauan, *Organs and Pianos,* p. 181.
7. RSK III interview.
8. Hauan, *Organs and Pianos,* p. 181.
9. Shari Kerr interview.
10. RSK III interview.
11. Ibid.
12. *The Daily Oklahoman,* January 8, 1963.
13. Hauan, *Organs and Pianos,* p. 185.
14. Fred R. Harris, *Potomac Fever* (New York: W.W. Norton & Company, 1977), p. 25, hereafter referred to as *Potomac Fever.*
15. *The Daily Oklahoman,* January 7, 1963.
16. Ibid.
17. Ibid., January 8, 1963.
18. Ibid.
19. *Potomac Fever,* p. 30.
20. Ibid.
21. Bill Kerr interview.
22. *The Daily Oklahoman,* April 18, 1963.
23. Ibid.
24. Ibid., April 23, 1963.
25. *Potomoc Fever,* p. 41.
26. *The Daily Oklahoman,* May 20, 1964.
27. Hauan, *Organs and Pianos*, p. 188.

CHAPTER 6: LIGHTING A NEW TORCH
1. Jack T. Conn, *One Man In His Time* (Oklahoma City: Oklahoma Heritage Association, 1979), p. 141.
2. Ibid., p. 142.
3. Ibid.
4. *The Daily Oklahoman,* February 2, 1963.
5. Ibid.
6. Bill Kerr interview.
7. Ibid.
8. Ibid.
9. *The Daily Oklahoman,* December 7, 1963.
10. Ibid., December 30, 1963.
11. Ibid., August 14, 1964.
12. Ibid., June 4, 1965.
13. Ibid., August 20, 1965.
14. Ibid., January 2, 1966.
15. Ibid., January 20, 1967.
16. Ibid.
17. Ibid., January 26, 1967.
18. Ibid.
19. Jim Anderson interview.
20. Ibid.
21. Ibid.

CHAPTER 7: WATER CHAMPION
1. *The Daily Oklahoman,* September 8, 1964.

ENDNOTES **259**

2. Archives of the Water Development Foundation of Oklahoma, Inc., Oklahoma City, Oklahoma, hereafter referred to as Water Development Foundation Archives.
3. Archives of Oklahoma Water, Incorporated, Oklahoma City, Oklahoma, hereafter referred to as Oklahoma Water, Inc. Archives.
4. Ibid.
5. *The Daily Oklahoman,* February 24, 1967.
6. Ibid., June 24, 1967.
7. Oklahoma Water, Inc. Archives.
8. Ibid.
9. Ibid.
10. Ibid.
11. Ibid.
12. *The Daily Oklahoman,* February 28, 1967.
13. Ibid., January 23, 1972.
14. *Oklahoma City Times* (Oklahoma City, Oklahoma), March 8, 1971.
15. *The Waternaut,* newsletter of the Oklahoma Water Users Association, August, 1969.
16. Ibid.
17. Ibid.
18. Ibid., October, 1969.
19. Ibid.
20. Ibid.
21. Ibid., October, 1970.
22. Ibid., October, 1971.
23. *The Daily Oklahoman,* January 2, 1972.
24. Ibid., August 11, 1968.
25. 1977 U.S. Corps of Engineers report, p. 1-2.
26. McClellan-Kerr Arkansas River Navigation System, Recent Developments, June, 1977, Heritage Archives.
27. Ibid.
28. Ibid.
29. *Oklahoma Journal* (Midwest City, Oklahoma), June 23, 1971.

CHAPTER 8: LOU
1. Ibid.
2. Ibid.
3. Ibid.
4. Ibid.
5. Ibid.

CHAPTER 9: THE GLOVER DEBATE
1. Oklahoma Water, Inc. Archives.
2. Ibid.
3. Ibid.
4. Ibid.
5. *Oklahoma Water, Incorporated* monthly newsletter, August, 1974.
6. *The Daily Oklahoman,* May 3, 1972.
7. Ibid.
8. Bob Kerr Jr. speech from Oklahoma Water, Inc. Archives.
9. Ibid.
10. *Broken Bow News* (Broken Bow, Oklahoma), May 10, 1972.
11. *The Daily Oklahoman,* May 3, 1972.
12. Ibid.
13. Oklahoma Water Inc. Archives.
14. *Mangum Star* (Mangum, Oklahoma), March 25, 1971.
15. *The Granite Enterprise* (Granite, Oklahoma), March 18, 1971.
16. Oklahoma Water, Inc. Archives.
17. *The Daily Oklahoman,* March 22, 1972.
18. Letter from Robert S. Kerr, Jr. to members of Water Development Foundation, Inc., March 10, 1972, Heritage Archives.
19. Letter from Peter Dominick to Don Maughan, February 7, 1972, Heritage Archives.

CHAPTER 10: DEVELOPING A WATER PLAN
1. Oklahoma Water, Inc. Archives.
2. *The Waternaut,* April, 1973.
3. Oklahoma Water Inc. Archives.
4. *The LeFlore County Sun* (Poteau, Oklahoma), August 26, 1973.
5. Ibid.
6. *Tulsa Tribune* (Tulsa, Oklahoma), April 24, 1972.
7. Ibid.
8. Oklahoma Water Inc. Archives.
9. Letter from Larkin Warner to Ronn Cupp, March 7, 2005.

10. Minutes of annual OWI meeting, October 25, 1973, OWI Archives.
11. Ibid.
12. Oklahoma Water, Inc. Archives.
13. Ibid.
14. 1978 special report of Oklahoma Water, Inc.
15. Ibid.
16. Phase I—Comprehensive Water Plan, draft copy, April 15, 1975.
17. Ibid.
18. Ibid.
19. Ibid.
20. Ibid.
21. Ibid.
22. *The Daily Oklahoman*, September 22, 1976.

CHAPTER 11: WATER FOR ECONOMIC DEVELOPMENT

1. Position paper, Oklahoma Water Inc. and Robert S. Kerr, November 11, 1975, Oklahoma Water Inc. Archives.
2. Ibid.
3. Ibid.
4. Ibid.
5. Oklahoma Water Inc. Archives.
6. Ibid.
7. Ibid.
8. Ibid.
9. *The Daily Oklahoman*, May 11, 1977.
10. Ibid.
11. *Oklahoma Monthly* (Ponca City, Oklahoma), December, 1977.
12. Oklahoma Water Inc. Archives.
13. Letter from David L. Boren to Senator Gene Howard and Speaker William Willis, June 30, 1977, Heritage Archives.
14. Oklahoma Water Inc. Archives.
15. Letter from Henry Bellmon to Robert S. Kerr, Jr., May 17, 1977, Heritage Archives.
16. Ibid.
17. Printed statement of Robert S. Kerr, Jr., February 22, 1977, Oklahoma Water Inc. Archives.
18. Ibid.
19. Letter from Robert S. Kerr, Jr. to President Jimmy Carter, July 12, 1977, Heritage Archives.
20. *Coalgate Record/Register*, November 17, 1977.
21. Inaugural address of Governor George Nigh, January, 1979, Heritage Archives.
22. Excerpts from Water Resources Policy Statement, 1979, Oklahoma Water Inc. Archives.
23. Oklahoma Water Inc. Archives.
24. Ibid.
25. Remarks of Robert S. Kerr, Jr., to National Waterways Conference, September 18, 1979, Oklahoma Water Inc. Archives.
26. Ibid.

CHAPTER 12: QUEST FOR THE SENATE

1. www.kiralaw.com
2. *The Daily Oklahoman*, April 17, 1979.
3. Ibid., May 18, 1980.
4. *The Daily Oklahoman*, July 2, 1980.
5. Ibid., June 26, 1980.
6. Interview with Melvin Moran, December 17, 2004, Heritage Archives.
7. *The Daily Oklahoman*, August 21, 1980.
8. Ibid., July 24, 1980.
9. Letter from Andrew M. "Andy" Coats to Bob Burke, February 15, 2005, hereafter referred to as Andy Coats letter, Heritage Archives.
10. Ibid.
11. *The Daily Oklahoman*, August 27, 1980.
12. Ibid.
13. Ibid.
14. Ibid., August 28, 1980.
15. Ibid.
16. Andy Coats letter.
17. Ibid.
18. Ibid.
19. *The Daily Oklahoman*, August 28, 1980.
20. Andy Coats letter.
21. Letter from Larry Joplin to Bob Burke, March 30, 2005, Heritage Archives.
22. *The Daily Oklahoman*, September 10, 1980.
23. Ibid.
24. Ibid.

25. Ibid., September 12, 1980.
26. Ibid., September 14, 1980.
27. Ibid., September 17, 1980.
28. *The Daily Oklahoman,* September 17, 1980.
29. Andy Coats letter.
30. Ibid.
31. Ibid.

CHAPTER 13: THE 1980 WATER PLAN
1. 1995 Update of the Oklahoma Comprehensive Water Plan, p. 4.
2. RSK III interview.
3. Transcript of Robert S. Kerr, Jr.'s speech to the Governor's Water Conference, December 15, 1980, Oklahoma Water Inc. Archives.
4. *The Daily Oklahoman,* December 16, 1980.
5. Letter from Robert S. Kerr, Jr. to OWI members, January 12, 1981, Oklahoma Water Inc. Archives.
6. RSK III interview.
7. 1995 Update of the Oklahoma Comprehensive Water Plan, p. 4.
8. Ibid.
9. Interview with James "Jim" Barnett, December 21, 2004, hereafter referred to as Jim Barnett interview, Heritage Archives.
10. Interview with Patty Eaton, September 21, 2005, Heritage Archives.
11. Interview with Aubrey Kerr, December 21, 2004, hereafter referred to as Aubrey Kerr interview, Heritage Archives.
12. Bob Burke, *Good Guys Wear White Hats: The Life of George Nigh.* Oklahoma City: Oklahoma Heritage Association (2000), p. 290.
13. Interview with Frank McPherson, December 21, 2004, hereafter referred to as Frank McPherson interview, Heritage Archives.
14. Ibid.
15. Ibid.
16. Ibid.
17. Ibid.
18. *The Daily Oklahoman,* November 12, 1984.
19. Ibid., January 20, 1984.
20. Ibid.
21. Undated document titled "Ten Year Goals for Major Emphasis," from files of Oklahoma Water, Inc.
22. Letter from Dean Schirf to Bob Burke, September 23, 2005, Heritage Archives.

CHAPTER 14: AN ACTIVE ADVOCATE
1. Interview with Richard Poole, December 20, 2004, hereafter referred to as Richard Poole interview, Heritage Archives.
2. Ibid.
3. Ibid.
4. Ibid.
5. Letter from Larkin Warner to Ronn Cupp, March 7, 2005, Heritage Archives.
6. www.kerrcenter.com
7. www.FDNcenter.org
8. Ibid.
9. www.thekerrfoundation.org
10. Lou Kerr interview.
11. Ibid.
12. Ibid.
13. Bill Ross interview.
14. www.kiralaw.com
15. Lou Kerr interview.
16. Ibid.
17. Ibid.
18. Letter from Robert S. Kerr, Jr., to Dr. Jerald C. Walker, December 5, 1985, Heritage Archives.
19. Interview with Rennard Strickland, December 8, 2004, Heritage Archives.
20. Ibid.
21. Ibid.
22. Ibid.
23. *The Daily Oklahoman,* May 22, 2002.
24. Ibid., April 14, 2003.
25. Oklahoma Hall of Fame file, Heritage Archives.
26. Ibid.
27. *The Daily Oklahoman,* January 30, 2004.
28 Ibid.
29. Ibid.
30. Ibid., February 3, 2004.
31. Lou Kerr interview.

95th Division Artillery 69

Ables, Angela 242
Ada Lions Club 23
Adair, Bob 237
Adair, Grayce Kay Kerr 29-30, 35, 38-39, 49, 53, 55, 67, 111, 135, 224, 227, 235-237
Air Force Association 103
Albert, Carl 128, 135, 149, 153, 157, 197
Alexander, Frank 194
Allied Arts 218
Allied Arts Foundation 241
Alpha Chi Omega 65
American Bar Association 247
American Cancer Society 102
American Legion 22-23
American Water Works Association 115
Anderson & Kerr Drilling Company 26, 28
Anderson, James K. "Jim" 42-48, 65, 67, 109, 140, 229-230, 256
Anderson, James Leroy 25-26, 29
Anderson, Jerrie 229-230
Anderson, L.W. 185
Anderson, Marilynne 140
Anderson, Mildred 47-48
Arcadia Lake 114, 119-121, 150, 183-185, 212
Arkansas Basin Development Association 120, 133, 160, 162, 172
Arkansas Basin Interstate Committee 179
Arkansas River 56-61, 74, 76-78
Atkinson, W.P. "Bill" 94

Badger, John Jr. 103
Baggett, Bryce 170
Baker, Bobby 106, 109
Baker, Loren 196
BancOklahoma 223
Banowski, William 196
Barnett, James 217, 242
Bartlett, Dewey 135, 157, 170
Basswood Lodge 32
Battle of Bunker Hill 56
Battle of Culloden 10
Beard, David 185
Bellmon, Henry 102, 123, 157, 192, 240
Bender, W.E. 160
Bengston, L.H. 137, 139
Benham-Blair and Affiliates 123
Bennett, Henry 38
Bernard, Spencer 172
Birch Lake 150
Bishop Angie Smith Chapel 253
Black Angus Motel 171
Blake, Bruce P. 254
Blake, Ernest E. 58-61
Blinn, C.J. 97
Boehler, Orlie 184
Boggy Depot 12, 18-19
Bonner, Cheryl 156
Borders, Johnny 196
Borelli, Gerald 157
Boren, David L. 12, 173, 182
Boren, Lyle H. 12
Boren, William 12
Boylan, Lisa 237
Boylan, Margaret "Moni" Kerr 27, 29, 43-44, 140, 224, 230, 237
Boylan, Tani 140
Bradshaw, A.E. 105
Breene, Blanche 23
Breene, Harry 23
Broken Bow Lake 150

Broken Bow Lake Association 185
Brooks, William 185
Brown, John A. 58
Browne, Virgil 85
Bryan, Billy 204
Brydia, Catherine 38
Bureau for Business and Economic Research 171
Bureau of Reclamation 155, 165, 183
Burk, Gil 196
Buttram, Frank 61

Callaham, Jewel 156
Campbell, Lillie 225, 237
Canton Lake 62
Cantwell, Sarah Frances 29
Capitol Hill Beacon 121
Capitol Hill High School 139
Capps, Gilmer 170
Cargill, O.A. 58
Carter, Jimmy 187-188, 203
Castleberry, Ann 147
Castleberry, Bert 121, 147, 158-160, 171-172
Caucus on Eastern Oklahoma's Future 168, 180
Central Oklahoma Project 114-117, 119-121, 161
Central State University 184
Chastain, Bill 239
Choctaw Nation 18
Chouteau, A.F. 76
Christian Science 44, 47
Church, Lloyd E. 82, 121, 124, 157, 170
Churchill, Winston 50, 107, 162
Cimino Bay 32

Cities Service Company 168
Civil War 11
Clark, Gene 36
Clark, Lori 237
Clark, Lowell 32
Claudius I 119
Clegg, Billy Joe 196
Clingman, Mike 197
Coalgate Record/Register 123, 186
Coats, Andrew M. "Andy" 191-208
Cody, Harvey 65, 67
Cody, Harvey Jr. 67
Cody, Thelma 67
Coker, Betty 147
Coker, Dirk 147
Coker, Lem Z. 137
Coker, Manolia Mae 137
Colbert's Ferry 12
Coltrane Road 39-40
Committee for a Responsible Budget 243
Conn, Jack T. 97-98
Cooper, Leroy Gordon 103
Copelin, Farrell 121
Corbett, Luke R. 8
Cornelsen, Wayman 179
Cotner, Howard 123, 170
Cotton Electric Coop 123
Council of Soil Conservation Districts 157
Cox, Barbour 170
Cox, Beverly 218
Crable, A.L. 38
Crain, Bill 197, 204
Crawford, Ann 227, 230
Crawford, Bill 230
Crockett, Bernice 123-126, 168-170, 179, 186
Cromley, Allan 94
Crow, Herschal 170, 172, 211

Crowe, V.P. 157
Cunningham, Jacques 160
Cunningham, Morrison B. 115
Cupp, Ronn W. 162-163, 177, 179, 181, 192, 197, 213

D'Andriole, Anna 218
Dahl, John 170
Daly, Edward G. 77
Dean A. McGee Eye Institute 241
Deep Fork Creek 119-120, 184
Deering, Ferdie 179
DeGreer, Myron 121
Democratic National Convention 38
Denison Dam 62
Derryberry, Larry 204
Dierks Forests, Inc. 123
Dillon, Dick 121
Doughty, Nelson 179
Douglas, William O. 121
Downs, George Jr. 179
Draper, Stanley 61-62
Dresner, Morris and Tororello 201
Duke, R.P. 123
Dulaney, Tom 157
Duncan, Burton 123

East Central Normal School 22
East Central State College 147
East Central State University 196
Eaton, Patty 217
Eddy, Mary Baker 44, 47
Edmondson, Ed 88-92, 121, 123, 128, 153, 160
Edmondson, J. Howard 88-92
English, Paul 196

Erhard, Ludwig 101
Fears, Rufus 254
Ferrell, Don 170
Fidelity Bank N.A. 99-100, 193, 223
Fidelity National Bank 106, 126
Fidelity of Oklahoma, Inc. 223
Field, Larry 117
Field, Leon 117, 170
First Baptist Church 39, 88, 90
First State Bank of Gould 123
Flaigg, Norman 121
Flood Control Act of 1936
Flynn, Olney 101
Fore, Jim 11
Fore, Margaret 11-14
Fore, Sam 11
Fort Cobb Reservoir 150
Fort Gibson Lake 62-63, 129
Fort Gibson Lake Association 185
Fort Sill, OK 67
Forum on Domestic Policy 177
Foss Reservoir 150
Funston, Bob 179, 192

Gamel, Bill 215
Gannaway, Charles B. Jr. 160
Gary, Raymond 101, 173
Gates, George H. 160
Gaut, Marvin 109
Gaylord, E.K. 58, 85
Glover Creek 57, 149-157, 183-184
Goals for Central Oklahoma Council 223
Goldwater, Barry 101
Gould, Charles 58
Governor's Water Conference 214
Governor's Water Study Committee 82
Graham, Gar 196
Graham, Newton T. 74, 77, 79
Grand Lake 62
Grand Lake Association 185
Grand River 129
Grand River Dam Authority 62
Grand, L.W. Jr. 160
Grayce B. Kerr Fund 238
Great Depression 30, 56
Great Salt Plains 62
Green, George H.C. 105
Grubb, Herbert 214
Gulf of Mexico 118, 158
Guthrie Chamber of Commerce 62
Guymon Chamber of Commerce 123

Hadley, Garland 146
Hall, Artie 12, 15
Hall, David 160, 166, 172-173, 204
Hall, Joe 215
Hall, Polk 16, 20
Hamilton, Dick 179
Hamilton, James 196, 202
Haney, Enoch Kelly 218
Hannah, John 163
Harbour, T. Elmer 74
Hardwick, Kermit 157
Harlow's Weekly 59
Harrill, Thomas C. 61
Harris, Fred 92-95, 101-102, 128, 135,154
Hart, Dan 229
Hart, Elizabeth Kay 250
Hart, Gary 207
Hart, Mary Grayce 250
Hart, Valerie Kay Kerr 66-75, 144, 228-230, 237, 250
Hartmann, Jeff 242
Haskell, Charles 77
Hauan, Marty 95
Hawks, Rex 90
Hayes, Amos 19
Hays, Burl 91
Henderson, George 247
Henry Hitch Farms 123
Henry, Patrick 10
Heyburn Reservoir 63
High Plains Study Council 182
Highland Park United Methodist Church 145
Hill, George 123, 186
Hilton Inn West 205
Hinds, H.I. 90
Hitch, H.C. Jr. 117
Hitch, Paul 179
Holden, C.R. 179
Hood, David 191
Hooper, Roy 205, 213
Horne, James 235
Howard, Gene 182, 196, 201-202
Howell, Dorothy 126
Hudson Lake 129, 150
Hugo Lake 150
Hulah Lake 62-63
Hunter, Blanche 156
Huntley, Chet 85

Illinois River 129
Indian Territory 16-19
Inhofe, James 196
Irvine, Francis S. 193, 242

Jackson, LeRoy 184
Jade Boutique 139
Jenson, John 246
Johnson Hall 156
Johnson, Lady Bird 135
Johnson, Lyndon 85, 88,

101, 106-107, 111, 113, 135
Jones, Jackie 67
Jones, James 111
Joplin, Howard W. 196
Joplin, Larry 204
Junkin, Dan 146
Kaw Lake Association 185
Keesee, Paul 98
Keith, Guy N. 115, 121, 157, 162
Kelly, James J. 223
Kelly, Mike 197, 204
Kenneck, George 61
Kennedy, Donald S. 85
Kennedy, John F. 88-92, 101
Kermac Ranch 103
Kerr Aviation 126
Kerr Center 196
Kerr Center for Sustainable Agriculture 235-238
Kerr Foundation 99, 127, 146-147, 171, 193, 234-241, 244-245
Kerr Lounge 252
Kerr Pause 233
Kerr, Aubrey M. 25, 27, 30, 90, 140, 217, 227, 230
Kerr, Billy B. 25
Kerr, Breene Mitchell 26, 29, 30, 34, 37, 49, 53, 55, 65, 67, 92, 111, 140, 142, 238
Kerr, Carolyn 230
Kerr, Charlotte 237
Kerr, Cody Travis 66-75, 144, 230, 237, 247
Kerr, Conn and Davis 192
Kerr, Davis, Irvine, Krasnow, Rhodes and Semtner 99
Kerr, Elizabeth Hixson 237, 248, 251
Kerr, Geraldine 26, 53
Kerr, Grayce Breene 23-37, 234
Kerr, Irvine & Rhodes 192
Kerr, Irvine, Rhodes & Ables 242
Kerr, James Austin 248, 251
Kerr, Jewell 26-27, 30, 53, 224, 230, 237
Kerr, Joffa 140, 230
Kerr, John 10
Kerr, Katie 226, 228, 237
Kerr, Kiersten Frances 237, 248
Kerr, Laura 228, 237
Kerr, Lou Coker 137-147, 192-194, 200-201, 209, 220, 225, 228-231, 233-234, 237-241, 248, 253, 255, 257
Kerr, Margaret Churchel Wright 15-22
Kerr, Marilyn LaMoyne Cody 65-71, 237
Kerr, Mike 230
Kerr, Mildred Margaret 21
Kerr, Nancy 140, 227, 229-230
Kerr, Robert Samuel Sr. 19-95
Kerr, Robert Samuel III 32, 65-75, 91, 144, 191-193, 211, 213-216, 237, 248
Kerr, Robert Samuel IV 237, 248
Kerr, Robert Samuel Jr., childhood 26-48; college 65-71; early water development 113-163; U.S. Senate campaign 191-209; state water plan 165-175, 211-216
Kerr, Sharon LaMoyne "Shari" 66-75, 140, 144, 149, 226, 228, 237, 247-248, 252
Kerr, Shelley 230
Kerr, Sherry 218
Kerr, Sheryl 238
Kerr, Sir Robert 9
Kerr, Steven Cris 139-146, 237, 248, 252
Kerr, Travis Mitchell 21, 25
Kerr, William Edward 10-11
Kerr, William Graycen "Bill" 29-30, 53, 55, 87, 94, 100, 109, 111, 135, 140, 142, 227, 230, 237-238
Kerr, William Rogers "Billy" 66-75, 104, 140, 144, 237, 247
Kerr, William Samuel 11-22, 27
Kerr, Wilson Hixson 248
Kerr-McGee Corporation 29, 100, 193, 220-222, 253
Kerr-McGee Industries 109
Kerr-McGee Oil Industries 99
Keystone Lake 128
Kidd, Bob Lee Jr. 167
King Edward I 10
King Henry I 10
King, Don Arch 121, 157
Kirkpatrick, Glade R. 160, 179
Klabzuba, Richard W. 196
Knott, Brenda 229
Korean War 69
Kost, J.H. 48
Ku Klux Klan 11

KWTV 139
Lake Carl Blackwell 62
Lake Eufaula 120-121, 150
Lake Eufaula Association 185
Lake Keystone 150
Lake Murray 62
Lake of the Arbuckles 150
Lake Stanley Draper 115
Lake Tenkiller 63, 129
Lake Tenkiller Association 185
Lake Texoma 62-63
Lake Texoma Association 185
Lake Thunderbird 150
Land, Wood & Water 55, 155
Laney, Ben T. 74
Larson, James 185
Lawtonian Hotel 121
Lay, R. Thomas 242
Lee Creek 57
Leflore County Sun 167
Lewis, Mrs. Frank 156
Little River 57, 151
Lou C. Kerr Endowed Chair in Biomedical Research 246
Lucky, Grayson L. 254
Lukfata Lake 149-157, 162, 183-184
Lungrin, George 117

Madison, James 10
Mann, Raymond 117
Markham Ferry 62
Massachusetts Institute of Technology 235
Mayo Clinic 243
Mayo, John D. 77, 160
Maze, Maureen 67
McBride, Donald O. 74, 77-79, 81-82, 133, 155
McCall, S.K. 123
McCarty, J.D. 90

McClellan-Kerr Arkansas River Navigation Project 73-80, 120-131, 212
McClendon, Aubrey 230
McClendon, Carole 227, 237
McClendon, Joe 230, 237
McClendon, Katie 230
McClendon, Nancy 230
McCurtain Gazette 151
McDaniel, Tom 254
McFarlin Memorial Methodist Church 65
McGee Creek 212
McGee Creek Reservoir 114, 183-185
McGee, Dean A. 7, 29, 88, 91, 97-99, 223
McGee, Frank 85
McKee, Marvin 117, 170
McKeel, J.F. 22
McNeer, H.A. 105
McNeil, H.W. 94
McPherson, Frank 222
McSpadden, Clem 170
Melton, Michael R. 175
Mildren, Richard 197, 204, 253
Miller, George 170
Miller, Robert A. 242
Mississippi River 55-56, 167
Mississippi River Valley 61-62
Mitchell, Leona 254
Mitchell, Mary 11, 14
Mitchell, Rube 14
Monroe, Jim 151
Monroney, Mike 111, 128
Moore, Preston J. 102
Moran, Melvin 200
Morgan, Anne Hodges 146
Morgan, Mary Kimball 47
Morrell, Ralph 209
Morris, John 155
Morris, Richard 201
Morrison, John 105
Muddy Boggy Creek 183
Murphy, Robert 170, 197

National Academy of Public Administration 243
National Cowboy Hall of Fame 241
National Flood Insurance Program 216
National Reclamation Association 82
National Savings and Trust Company 106
National Waterways Conference 161, 188
Nelson, Forrest 121, 173
Nesbitt, Charles 197
New Mexico Military Institute 44-48, 162, 244
Nichols Hills United Methodist Church 254
Nickles, Don 196, 202, 205-208
Nigh, George 88-92, 135, 187, 192, 213-215, 217
Nixon, Richard 129, 131, 161, 177, 185-186
Noble, Ed 196
Norman, Lois 126
Norris, David 185
Norris, Harold 154
North Canadian River 58
Northhome 30-35

Odell, Jack 121
Ogallala formation 182, 186
Ogle, David 249
Ogle, Jackson David 231,

251
Ogle, James 231
Ogle, Laura Dyanne Kerr 139-146, 228, 231, 247, 249, 252
Ogle, Taylor Nicole 231, 249
Oklahoma 2000 243
Oklahoma A & M College 38
Oklahoma Arts Institute 241
Oklahoma Baptist University 22
Oklahoma Bar Association 100
Oklahoma Basins Project 155
Oklahoma City Art Museum 241
Oklahoma City Chamber of Commerce 57-62, 100, 115, 120, 135, 193, 223-234
Oklahoma City National Memorial 241
Oklahoma City University 243-246, 253-254
Oklahoma Comprehensive Water Plan 172-175, 212-217
Oklahoma Conservation Commission 62, 82
Oklahoma Court of Civil Appeals 204
Oklahoma Educational Television Authority 241
Oklahoma Gas and Electric Company 85, 242
Oklahoma Hall of Fame 246-247
Oklahoma Heritage Association 241, 246-247
Oklahoma Journal 129
Oklahoma Medical Research Foundation 246
Oklahoma Monthly 181
Oklahoma Municipal Improvements Authority 115
Oklahoma National Guard 22
Oklahoma Press Association 169
Oklahoma Society of Professional Engineers 115
Oklahoma State Chamber of Commerce and Industry 243
Oklahoma State University 166, 234, 238
Oklahoma Tax Commission 223
Oklahoma United Methodist Church Foundation 243
Oklahoma Water Council on Education 126, 168
Oklahoma Water Development Authority 180
Oklahoma Water Resources Board 82-84, 113, 157, 171-173, 179-181, 212-215, 242
Oklahoma Water Users Association 121, 123, 132, 158
Oklahoma Water, Incorporated 114-118, 125-131, 149-155, 157-162, 168-174, 185-186, 212-217
Oklahoma Weather Modification Advisory Committee 179
Old Texas Road 18
Oologah Lake 150
Optima Reservoir 62, 150
Orange Bowl 88
Otis Elevator Company 109
Overholser, Ed 61
Overstreet-Kerr Historical Farm 238
Ozark Plateau 57

Parks, David 246
Parris, Bob 179
Paul, William G. 247
Pearson, Drew 99
Pecan Valley 18, 87
Pelican Lake 30, 32, 36
Penn Square Bank 222
Pensacola Dam 62
Petitt, Ben 121
Phi Delta Theta 65
Phillips, Milt 123
Pick, Lewis A. 77
Pickens, Boone 247
Pine Creek Lake 150
Pinkey, Vernon W. 128, 160
Pittinger, Jim 157
Planning and Resources Board 82
Playboy 121
Poole, Richard 234
Port of Catoosa 129
Potomac Fever 92
Price, Christy 237
Price, Sandy 237
Privett, Rex 170
Public Works Administration 62
Pugh, Ed 213
Pummill, Loyd 121

Queen Elizabeth II 225

Raab, Frank 121, 173
Randle, Rodger 223
Randolph, Jennings 135
Reagan, Ronald 203, 206
Red Earth 241
Red River 57, 63, 151, 217
Red River Chloride

Control Project 216
Reed, Ada 19
Reed, William J. 19
Reserved Officers Training Corps 48
Revolutionary War 48
Reynolds, Bill 91
Rhodes, Horace G. 193, 233, 242
Rhodes, James W. 242
Rivers and Harbors Act 73
Robert S. and Grayce B. Kerr Foundation 238
Robert S. Kerr Jr. Chair in Natural Resources and Environmental Law 244
Robert S. Kerr Jr. Endowed Chair in Cancer Research 246
Robert S. Kerr Lock and Dam 127-128, 135
Robert S. Kerr Memorial Award 103
Robert S. Kerr Sr. Chair in Constitutional Law 244
Robert S. Kerr Water Research Center 114
Rockefeller, John D. 50
Rodman, Roland V. 85
Rogers, Will 162, 165
Roosevelt, Franklin D. 74, 159

Salvation Army 193, 209
Sandlin, Hugh 170
Sanguin, Wayne 170
Saunders, Orville 121, 157
Savage, Ted 121
Schirf, Dean 177
Science and Health with Key to the Scriptures 44
Senate Bill 215 212
Senate Bill 510 172

Senate Bill 625 180-181
Sewell, Frank 105
Shepherd Mall 139
Sheraton Century Center 214
Shotwell, Don 185
Skirvin Hotel 84
South Canadian River 58
Southeastern State College 126
Southwestern Stationery and Bank Supply 123
Spears, James 139
Special Committee on Water Development 205
Stallings, Thorne 196
Stamper, Joe 123
State Regents for Higher Education 241
State Street 39-40
Steed, Tom 111, 124
Steiger, John 168
Stewardship Ranch 235
Stewart, Bob 185
Stipe, Gene 170
Strasbaugh, Paul 120, 157, 162
Stratton, David 170
Stratton, Jess 121, 179
Strickland, Rennard 245
Sullivan, Glenn 213
Sullivant, Otis 93, 102
Sunset Bay 32
Swift and Company 123
Swisher, George 220
Swisher, Ginny 220
Symcox, Phil 123

Taylor, Frank 121
Taylor, James 10
Taylor, Zachary 10
Tennessee Valley Authority 82, 133
Texas County Irrigation Water Resources

Association 117
Texas Department of Water 215
The Daily Oklahoman 59, 80, 85, 94, 102, 181, 205, 253
The Farmer Stockman 59
The Kerr Foundation, Inc. 238-241
The Principia 47
Thoburn, Joseph B.
Thornton, Dwayne 246
Thornton, William 10
Tidwill, Courtney 121
Tilly, Joe 121
Tom Steed Lake 150
Tower, Marcus R. 160
Trapp, Martin E. 59
Trent, Paul E. 197
Trent, Ray 170
Truman, Harry S. 74
Tulsa Ballet Theatre 241
Tulsa Chamber of Commerce 79
Tulsa Tribune 168
Turner, Fred 179

United Founders Life Insurance Company 242
United States Army Corps of Engineers 56-57, 79-82, 115, 128, 160, 171, 215, 217
United States Army Reserve 69
United States Coast Guard 128
United States Department of Agriculture 182
United States Merchant Marine 48-49
United States Public Health Service 82, 113
United Way 100, 193
University of Central

Oklahoma 252
University of Oklahoma
12, 22, 65-69, 88, 92,
171, 196, 243
University of Texas 12, 18

vanden Heuvel, William J. 233, 247

Verdigris River 76

Waesche, Russell R. 128

Wagner, Stanley 147
Walker, Ginny 244
Walker, Jerald 244-245
Warner, Larkin 128, 162, 171, 235
Warren, Hugh 204
Warren, William K. Jr. 247
Washita River 58, 63
Water Development Financial Assistance Program 212
Water Development Foundation of Oklahoma 114-118, 162, 184
Water Development Revolving Fund 213-214
Water Resources Council 160-161, 178, 185
Water Resources Planning Act of 1965 83
Watkins, Wes 183-184
Waurika Lake 150
Webb, Roger 252
Webbers Falls Lake 150
Westbrook, Randy 151
Western Area Power Administration 215
Wharton, Mike 121
Whiteneck, Otho 123
Wichita River 217
Widener, Spuds 121
Wilkinson, Charles "Bud" 92, 101
William the Conqueror 10
Williams Companies 223
Williams, Edward Bennett 106
Williams, Penny 223
Willis, William P. 182
Wimberly, Carl 26
Wimberly, Lois Frances Kerr 18-19, 25
Winston, William 10
WKY-TV 85
World War II 74
Wright, Bryan 117
Wright, Fannie Taylor 16
Wright, James 121
Wright, John 121, 124
Wright, Moses Leonard 16

Young, Stanton L. 115

Zelnick, John 196

Zink, John 196, 202, 208